Oracle on VMware

From Laptops to Production

Oracle In-Focus Series

Bert Scalzo, PhD.

To my wife Susan – she's complained that every book I have written to date is dedicated to my dogs, so here's one for her.

Bert Scalzo, PhD.

Oracle on VMware

From Laptops to Production

By Bert Scalzo , PhD.

Copyright © 2008 by Rampant TechPress. All rights reserved.

Printed in the United States of America.

Published in Kittrell, North Carolina, USA.

Oracle In-focus Series: Book 29

Series Editor: Donald K. Burleson

Production Manager: Robin Rademacher

Editor: Valerre Aquitaine

Production Editor: Teri Wade

Cover Design: Janet Burleson

Printing History: September 2008 for First Edition

Oracle, Oracle7, Oracle8, Oracle8i, Oracle9i, Oracle10g and Oracle 11g are trademarks of Oracle Corporation.

Many of the designations used by computer vendors to distinguish their products are claimed as Trademarks. All names known by Rampant TechPress to be trademark names appear in this text as initial caps.

Flame Warriors illustrations are copyright © by Mike Reed Illustrations Inc.

The information provided by the authors of this work is believed to be accurate and reliable. However, because of the possibility of human error by our authors and staff, Rampant TechPress cannot guarantee the accuracy or completeness of any information included in this work and is not responsible for any errors, omissions, or inaccurate results obtained from the use of information or scripts in this work.

ISBN 10: 0-9797951-4-1
ISBN 13: 978-0-9797951-4-5
Library of Congress Control Number: 2008932387

Table of Contents

Using the Online Code Depot

Purchase of this book provides complete access to the online code depot that contains sample code scripts. Any code depot scripts in this book are located at the following URL in zip format and ready to load and use:

rampant.cc/oracle_vmware.htm

If technical assistance is needed with downloading or accessing the scripts, please contact Rampant TechPress at rtp@rampant.cc.

Conventions Used in this Book

It is critical for any technical publication to follow rigorous standards and employ consistent punctuation conventions to make the text easy to read. However, this is not an easy task. Within database terminology, there are many types of notation that can confuse a reader. For example, some Oracle utilities such as STATSPACK and TKPROF are always spelled in CAPITAL letters, while Oracle parameters and procedures have varying naming conventions in the database documentation. It is also important to remember that many database commands are case sensitive, and are always left in their original executable form, and never altered with italics or capitalization.

Hence, all Rampant TechPress books follow these conventions:

Parameters – All database parameters will be *lowercase italics*. Exceptions to this rule are parameter arguments that are commonly capitalized (KEEP pool, TKPROF), these will be left in ALL CAPS.

Variables – All procedural language (e.g. PL/SQL) program variables and arguments will also remain in *lowercase italics* (*dbms_job, dbms_utility*).

Tables & dictionary objects – All data dictionary objects are referenced in lowercase italics (*dba_indexes*, *v$sql*). This includes all *v$* and *x$* views (*x$kcbcbh, v$parameter*) and dictionary views (*dba_tables*, *user_indexes*).

SQL – All SQL is formatted for easy use in the code depot, and all SQL is displayed in lowercase. The main SQL terms (select, from, where, group by, order by, having) will always appear on a separate line.

Programs & Products – All products and programs that are known to the author are capitalized according to the vendor specifications (CentOS, VMware, Oracle, etc). All names known by Rampant TechPress to be trademark names appear in this text as initial caps. References to UNIX are always made in uppercase.

Acknowledgements

This type of highly technical reference book requires the dedicated efforts of many people. Even though we are the authors, our work ends when we deliver the content. After each chapter is delivered, several Oracle DBAs carefully review and correct the technical content. After the technical review, experienced copy editors polish the grammar and syntax.

The finished work is then reviewed as page proofs and turned over to the production manager, who arranges the creation of the online code depot and manages the cover art, printing distribution, and warehousing.

In short, the authors play a small role in the development of this book, and we need to thank and acknowledge everyone who helped bring this book to fruition:

Robin Rademacher, for the production management, including the coordination of the cover art, page proofing, printing, and distribution.

Teri Wade, for help in the production of the page proofs.

Janet Burleson, for exceptional cover design and graphics.

John Lavender, for assistance with the web site, and for creating the code depot and the online shopping cart for this book.

With my sincerest thanks,

Bert Scalzo, PhD.

Preface

We live in interesting times. Oracle continues to evolve into an ever greater database, as well as other software which also seems to continuously improve with no end in sight. But it is the new and cheaper hardware that really makes database administration options so interesting these days. Disk space has dropped to under .50 cents per gigabyte and memory costs are around $50 per gigabyte. Add to that sub-$200 quad core CPUs plus all the other cheap commoditized components and database server performance is staggering as compared to just a mere decade ago. Hence, newer technologies and techniques have now evolved to challenge established paradigms. Virtualization is one example and with rapid adoption and ever increasing usage, it is making its way into everything requiring a server.

The glorious gifts of the gods
are not to be cast aside.

Homer, The Iliad

Some people would argue that databases are still not a good match for virtualization since databases generally require direct access to the IO subsystem for best possible performance. But hardware is becoming so cheap and powerful that administrative costs and manageability issues are quickly becoming the metrics of greatest importance. The trend seems clear – virtualization is being liberally applied across the board.

This book is the result of nearly two years of experience in running Oracle 10g, 11g, and Real Application Clusters (RAC) on VMware. It is my belief that databases such as Oracle and SQL Server are going to be virtualized more and more, so this book's content will be very relevant!

Prologue

By Donald K. Burleson

The concept of virtual machines in not new and IBM mainframes have had the ability to "split" mainframe machines using tools such as Prism. In a nutshell, vmware allows the DBA to apportion hardware resources such as dedicated CPU, RAM, and disk as-if they were on a separate server. Of course, Oracle has other ways to dedicate CPU's, via the Oracle affinity feature for example, and adjust CPU dispatching priorities with the UNIX/Linux "nice" command.

In the world of minicomputers, vmware was largely ignored until manufacturers began to offer large machines such as the HP Superdome and UNISYS ES-700 series, which are large mainframe-like machines capable of supporting dozens of Oracle instances.

Now, with the 2nd age of mainframe computing arriving soon, these large monolithic servers can be split into "virtual machines," allowing one master OS to host many other operating systems within a single large server. Disk, CPU, and RAM are now fault-tolerant and redundant, making the monolithic approach very compelling to large corporations. This also makes Oracle vmware an important tool for multi-OS environments to achieve server consolidation.

Instead of small, independent servers, the major hardware vendors are pushing large servers with transparent sharing of hardware resources, coining the term "partitionable servers."

- **HP** - With scalability up to 64 processors, the HP Integrity Superdome Server.

- **Sun** - The largest Sun Starcat server has 128 CPU's and Solaris processor sets allow for virtualization. Solaris-based applications and Solaris™ containers are an integral part of Solaris 10.
- **IBM** - IBM now goes beyond the Regatta class servers with the P690, a behemoth with 128 processors. This allows Oracle shops to scale-up within the same server.
- **UNISYS** - The UNISYS ES-7000 series offers a 32 CPU server capable of running dozens of large Oracle applications.

Without server consolidation, the DBA had to deliberately over-allocate RAM and CPU resources to accommodate spikes in processing, which was a huge waste of hardware power.

Enter Oracle vmware

At Oracle OpenWorld 2007, Oracle announced new virtualization software, causing a firestorm of interest and a decline in competitor VMware's stock. Oracle VM, which can be downloaded free, is based on the Xen open-source hypervisor product. With all of the hype, Oracle managers are now struggling to understand how Oracle VM can fit into their enterprise. Let's explore how virtualization is becoming part of the 21st century database toolbox.

It's back to the future for the Oracle database world. The inefficient one server/one database approach of the 1990's client-server technology is long gone and Oracle shops are now re-consolidating their data resources, moving back to the mainframe-like centralization of the 1980's. While Oracle touts VM as a latest-and-greatest solution, we need to remember that server virtualization has been around for decades.

Virtualization is simply the partitioning of a server in order to host multiple OS environments. Whether it's running virtual

Windows on your Macintosh laptop or partitioning a 128 CPU mainframe, IT managers are leveraging virtualization solutions to consolidate multiple OS environments. At a high level, virtualization is the process of segregating server resources in a homogeneous environment, but it is most commonly used to host different operating systems within a single monolithic server -- and this is a step toward OS independence.

A brief history of Oracle virtualization

Oracle rose to dominate the database market primarily because of its ability to run on more than 60 platforms, everything from a mainframe to a Macintosh. However, Oracle soon faced the challenge of running multiple OS environments within the same server. In early 2005, Oracle announced that their version of VMWare would come pre-loaded with both Linux and Oracle, making it easier than ever to run Linux on a MS Windows server. Oracle then embraced the idea of server consolidation via the 11g Grid Initiative. At Openworld 2007, Oracle claimed that 99% of their customers run multiple instances within a single host machine and so began pushing the new VM product.

Although VM is free for download, support costs currently run $499/year for 1 or 2 CPU systems and $999/year for others. Thus far, VM is limited to Intel platforms, and will support only Linux and Windows servers. Oracle VM also offers a GUI management console, which his HTML-based, to allow easy management of both the overall OS and the virtual machines running under the master OS. Oracle is incorporating virtualization along several areas:

- **SOA** - Oracle plans to incorporate Oracle VM into their Fusion stack, allowing a method for unifying diverse applications onto a single server using SOAP. Oracle President Charles Phillips notes that Oracle VM will help SAP shops migrate from their foreign ERP's to Oracle Applications. "We want to help customers integrate their software with third-party applications made in Germany," he said at OpenWorld.

- **Consolidating heterogeneous environments** - Oracle VM is useful for shops that wish to consolidate different applications onto a single hardware platform. A common example is running Windows side-by-side with UNIX (HP/UX, Solaris, AIX, or Linux) on a large monolithic server. For example, instead of buying six 2 CPU servers, you can buy one 4 CPU 64-bit server with 16 GB RAM, and save a bundle of cash.
- **Oracle OLAP consolidation** – There are many benefits of running Oracle 10g R2 with virtualization with the Oracle Business Intelligence Suite (OLAP).
- **Oracle application server** - Oracle Application Server can be run with Oracle on a single server using VM.
- **Students** - Using virtualization is popular among people who want to learn RAC on a personal computer, whereby VM can allow a single server to mimic several RAC nodes.

Let's see how vmware solutions fit into the movement toward large consolidated server environments, the 2nd age of centralized mainframe computing.

The second age of mainframe computing

The early 21st century is seeing the second age of mainframe computing, a change away from the minicomputer hardware architectures of past decades. Instead of small, independent servers, the major hardware vendors are pushing large servers with transparent sharing of hardware resources, coining the term "partitionable servers."

Some general fallacies about the hazards of vmware consolidation include some common misconceptions:

- **Single point of failure fallacy** - Properly configured, none of these architectures suffers any single point of failure. Today's hardware has fully-redundant everything, and with geographical data replication (Streams, Dark Fiber RAC), hardware-related failures are becoming quite rare.
- **Rogue applications can "hog" a centralized computer** - Also, the segmentation of large computers into smaller, fully isolated slices had been done successfully for decades, and the system administrator has the ability to "fence" RAM and dedicate CPU's to specific applications using CPU affinity, the "nice" command, and setting *cpu_count* and *resource_manager_cpu_allocation*). Also, vmware solutions provide a similar solution for mixed OS environments.

But how does Oracle vmware fit into these existing virtualization techniques? There are some shortcomings of Oracle VM:

- **Unshared resources** - Server resources cannot be easily shared, and it counteracts the goal of server consolidation to leverage on a massive shared computing resource.
- **Measurable overhead** - We must remember that Oracle VM imposes some overhead, and a savvy DBA will always perform a workload benchmark using other alternatives such as containers, and para-virtualization before choosing virtualization.
- **Bad for the DBA job market** - Server consolidation is bad for the DBA job market because one of the main reasons for consolidating hardware resources is the savings from reducing DBA staff. A typical shop can save a million dollars a year by removing a dozen DBAs. The one-server/one-application paradigm has proven too expensive, so many enterprises are now moving back to the centralized architectures of old.

In sum, Oracle vmware fits nicely into the strategic plans for server consolidation but the savvy Oracle professional must recognize that virtualization has both benefits and limitations. It remains to be seen whether VM will become a permanent part of the data center, of if it will be only used as a stopgap tool for shops that want to run Windows in a Linux environment.

Introduction

CHAPTER 1

Oracle professionals demand the latest technology.

What is Virtualization?

Virtualization is simply software emulation of hardware resources that enables one physical machine to effectively function as several logical discrete machines. Since this abstraction is done at machine level, it is often referred to as *platform virtualization*. This concept has further been extended to virtualize specific system resources such as storage volumes, name spaces, and network resources. This is commonly called *resource virtualization*. While this book will explore both kinds of virtualization at various points, it is nonetheless primarily platform virtualization that is the central theme of this book. Thus, generic references to virtualization will always mean platform virtualization.

Code Depot Username = reader, Password = virtual

There are five kinds of platform virtualization technologies and products as highlighted below by Figure 1.1.

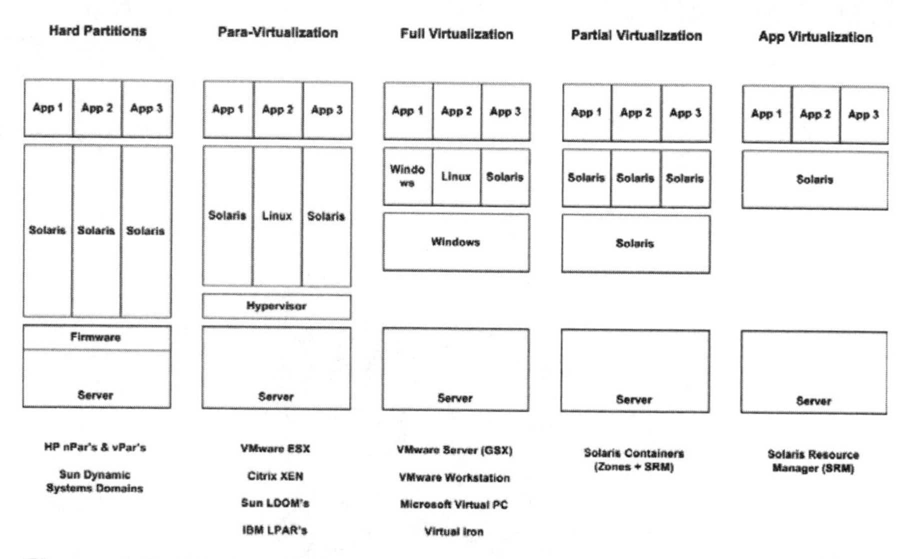

Figure 1.1: *Platform Virtualization Technologies*

This book will restrict itself to the first three platform virtualization technologies: Hard Partitions, Para-Virtualization and Full or Native Virtualization.

VMware Server and Microsoft Virtual PC are probably the best examples of Full (or Native) Virtualization and both products are free. Moving up the virtualization technology "food-chain," the products become increasingly expensive. VMware Workstation offers just a few more features than VMware Server and it currently costs about $170. Para-Virtualization products like VMware ESX range in price from $1,000 to almost $6,000 per two processors, however Sun's Logical Domains are free. Moreover, the Hard Partition Virtualization products' prices tend to be based on the hardware configuration (i.e. # CPU's) and neither the hardware nor the virtualization software in these enterprise class machines tends to be cheap.

Virtualization's Popularity

The meteoric rise in popularity of virtualization is nearly unheralded. In 2006, Gartner listed five of its top ten strategic technologies for 2007 to involve virtualization. Such preponderance in one category has never before or since occurred in their annual technology survey. Few information technologies have grown so quickly or had as optimistic a market potential as virtualization as shown below in Figure 1.2 by IDC's "Rise of Virtualization" projections.

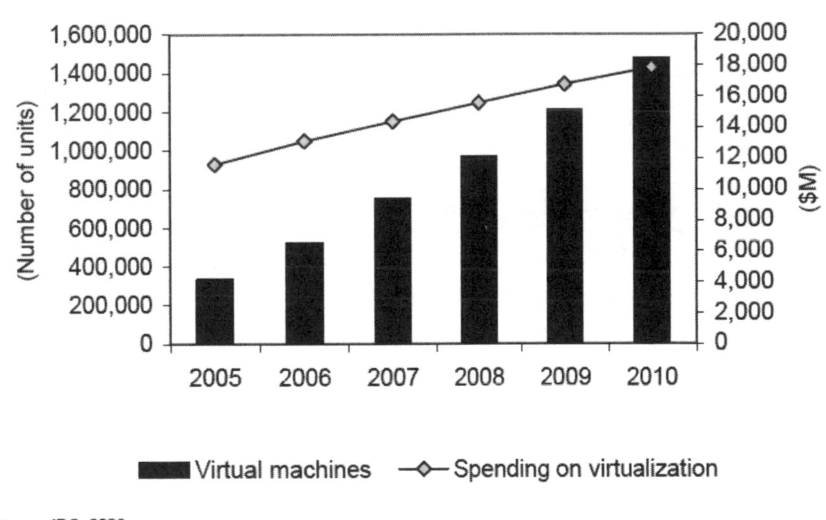

Figure 1.2: *IDC's The Rise of Virtualization*

If the virtualization market growing 350% in just five years is not astounding enough, then look at VMware's 2007 stock chart shown below in Figure 1.3. In just three months, this stock rose from its IPO price of $29 to over $104 – an amazing 260% growth in just three months! That is an astounding stock chart in the post tech-bubble bust. But virtualization is just that hot – and clearly here to stay.

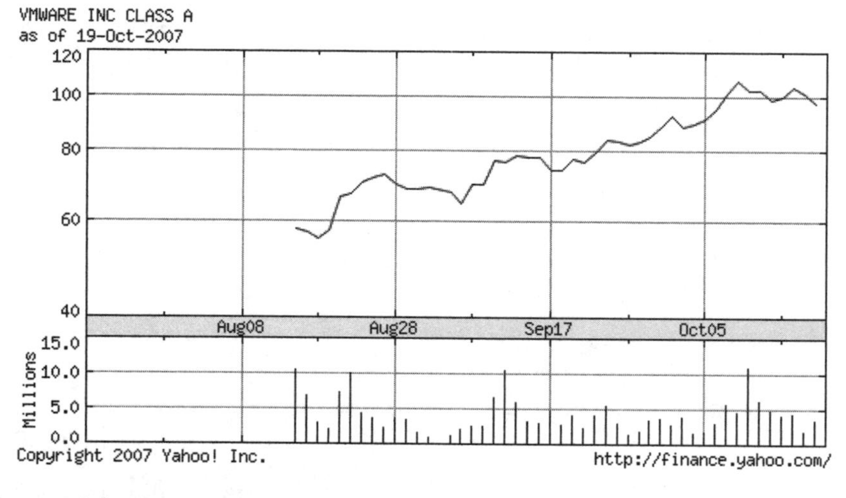

Figure 1.3: *VMWare Stock Chart*

Virtualization's Benefits

There are so many universally acknowledged benefits attributed to server virtualization that it is reasonably unnecessary to provide a complete and comprehensive list in this book. But the list below examines some of the more relevant advantages, especially as it potentially relates to Oracle databases.

- Lower IT Infrastructure Costs
- Improved Resource Utilization
- Greater Server Consolidation
- Enhanced High Availability
- Faster Disaster Recovery
- Using Virtual Appliances
- Better & Faster Provisioning

- Lower Power & Cooling Costs
- Reduce Server Room Space Needs
- Hardware and Image Independence

Do some of these points sound familiar? Maybe that is because Oracle's been working on improving along several of these criteria with their newer database technologies, such as RAC and Grid. Plus, Oracle's extensive platform support and features like cross-platform transportable tablespaces clearly target hardware independence. What that means is that both virtualization and Oracle's technology trends are quite harmonious. They are very clearly not at odds.

So system architects and database administrators should look for opportunities for these various technology solutions to augment, compliment, or supplant each other. And that is not a bad thing. It simply means that some problems and their solutions are best handled at various levels and not always within a specific technology such as within the database itself. For example, which scenario offers simpler new database deployment and provisioning?

Traditional Method

Operating System

- Install
- Patch
- Optimize

Database Software

- Install
- Patch
- Optimize

Database Itself

- Optimize init.ora or SPFile settings
- Create Database
- Define Initial -
- Disk Groups & Tablespaces
- Roles, Profiles, Policies & Resources
- Schemas, Tables, Indexes, Views, Code, etc
- Jobs, Programs, Classes, Schedules & Chains
- Grants, Contexts, Pub/Priv Synonyms & Links

Via Virtualization

Deploy Database Virtual Appliance

Virtualization Support

Both the hardware and software vendors are rapidly embracing virtualization. However, database vendors have been a bit slow to the dance. It could be that database vendors and DBAs believe that database tuning requires direct access and control over low level I/O subsystems for optimal performance. But if the hardware is say, ten times faster, what does a 10-20% overhead for virtualization matter?

Although Oracle's metalink has some documents which state that Oracle has not yet verified or certified the database for virtual machines, it has been the author's experience that virtualization abstraction does not impede nor complicate database deployment, management or tuning. In fact, it seems to simplify it. The only area that poses some additional questions/issues is backup and recovery. B&R has been complicated more by cheap hardware and hardware technologies such as RAID.

The real proof for support lies with the CPU vendors – both Intel and AMD have introduced virtualization support in their newer chip designs. With faster clock speeds and ever growing multi-core chips, resource utilization has become an important issue and most CPUs sit idle much of the time. Thus, server consolidation makes total sense; also, the space and power savings gain result in leaner and greener computing centers. With the proliferation of computing systems, these savings can be quite substantial. One recent article stated that the power savings alone in one company's experience paid for the entire cost of the reduced space needed. This clearly shows that secondary costs such as these are becoming more mission critical than hardware performance and direct costs. In fact, a 100-year old university found they could not upgrade their electrical systems in older buildings for their increasing computing needs. Therefore, power requirements alone were the new primary limiting factor in all future hardware purchase decisions.

Given the clear benefits and these leaner and greener trends, betting against virtualization going forward is not wise. It is not a luxury but, quite often, a necessity these days. And this will only increase with time.

Why VMware

So why choose VMware Server? The answer is simple: it is free, works flawlessly, is compatible with other non-free products, and VMware has something like a 70% market share. That means it is a perfect basis for a book. Not only can it be downloaded for free and used with the virtual appliance contained on the included DVD, but it is quite likely that current or future virtualization needs will utilize some VMware products.

That is not to say that other vendors' products are inferior in any way. In fact, since other products like Microsoft Virtual PC and Virtual Iron are free, they are also great candidates. However, VMware's popularity, hands down, makes the book universally more applicable. Note that most concepts or techniques mentioned within this book are similarly universal in nature. This means that they should apply, with minimal changes, to these other virtualization platforms as well.

Future Trends

I don't have a magic crystal ball or I would have made a few million in the market and retired already. But it seems clear that the trend is for increased virtualization at nearly every level.

Back in the mid-1960's and early 1970's, mainframes had sufficient excess CPU capacity that warranted the creation of virtual machines. For example, IBM's VM – which was the origin of the term *hypervisor.* Contemporary multi-core CPUs and cheap memory make even today's hungriest applications seem tame. So once again, spare or excess hardware capacity exists – even on lowly notebooks and laptops. It seems that there is as much a need for virtualization today as 40 years ago!

Also, today's database administrators and application developers need to work within ever complex and changing environments. Yet again, virtualization is the easiest way to conquer these challenges. Look for virtualization to become prolific and mainstream technology.

Oracle's Own VM

At Oracle Open World 2007, Oracle shocked quite a few people by announcing their own new virtual machine offering: Oracle VM. Oracle claims that it is up to three times faster than other server virtualization products. Now with their Enterprise Linux, Oracle VM, Oracle database, Automatic Storage Management (ASM), and the Oracle Cluster File System (OCFS), Oracle has truly become a robust and comprehensive vendor for database infrastructure. Moreover, with their recent applications space acquisitions, Oracle has become a genuine "one-stop-shop" for running large, scalable enterprise systems.

This book was already half written when Oracle VM debuted and besides, VMWare is a very likeable product. Referring again back to Figure 1.1, Oracle VM is nothing more than repackaging of the open-source based *Xen* offering (recently acquired by Citrix). It is just another hypervisor or *para-virtualization* solution whose core is based on a streamlined version of Linux. This is covered in more detail in Chapter 3. The Oracle VM User Guide displays its architecture as shown in Figure 1.4.

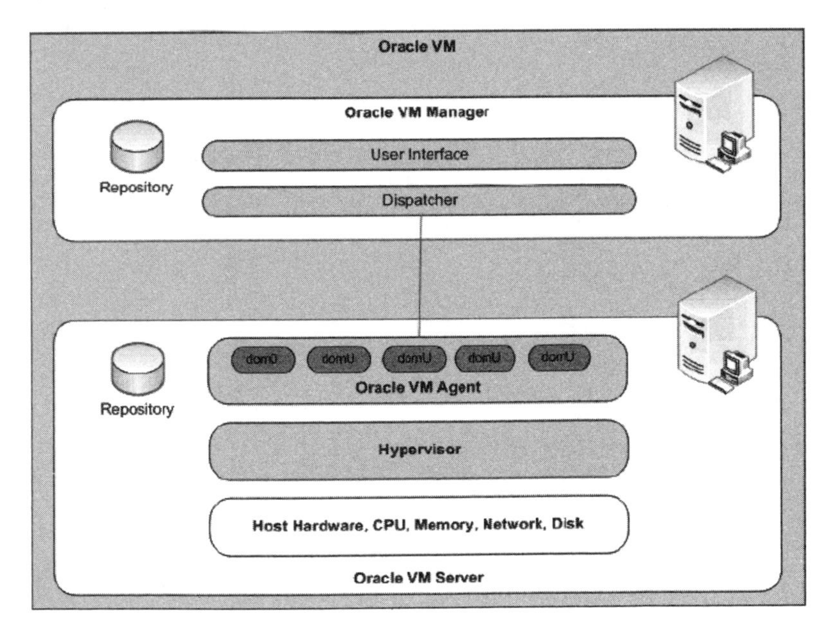

Figure 1.4: *Oracle VM Architecture*

Conclusion

There are many cost-related and resource-related benefits to be realized by using VM. Benefits can be realized in lower infrastructure costs, higher availability of resources, and faster disaster recovery. The meteoric growth of virtualization is unprecedented and a testament to the future of this technology. The next chapter covers the architecture of VM.

Architecture

CHAPTER

Always apply the appropriate technology.

Reasonable Choices

As was briefly pointed out in the prior chapter, there are at least five significantly different technologies for implementing virtualization. Each has their pros and cons, especially with respect to database performance or throughput. However, only two of them are the subject of this book: Paravirtualization and Full Virtualization, as shown below in Figure 2.1. The restriction was chosen for the simple reason that these technologies and products from VMware permit one to intermix and upgrade or downgrade between them as one sees fit. That is maximum flexibility and portability, which is always highly, if not most, desirable. Plus, it provides a single vendor solution that also happens to start as freeware for low-end servers and developer machines. Therefore, it offers higher market adoption and a commanding market share, both of which contribute to easier staffing. It is available on two of the most common operating systems: Windows and Linux.

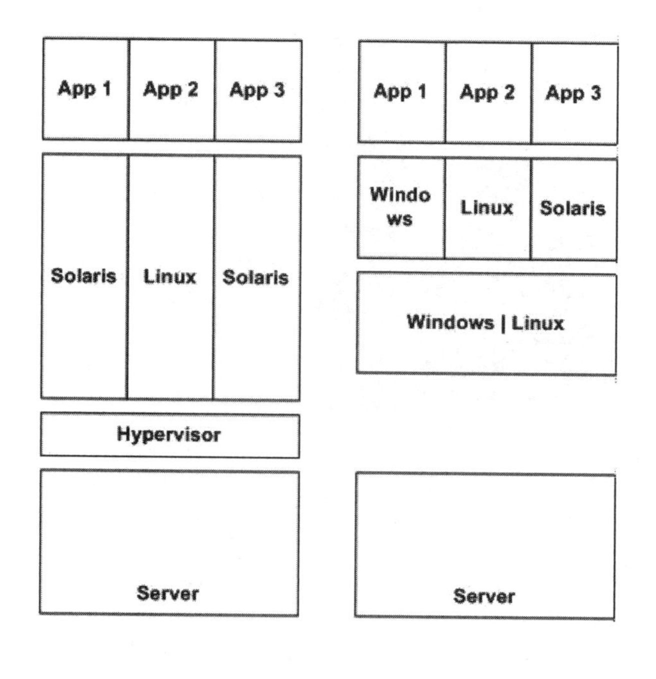

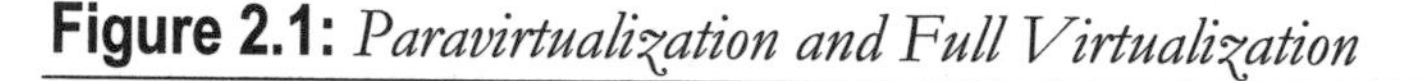
Figure 2.1: *Paravirtualization and Full Virtualization*

Contrary to popular belief, both these methods are really nothing more than software solutions that fundamentally accomplish nearly the same end result. In the case of VMware Server ESX, the hypervisor is really nothing more than their own radically pared down stand-alone operating system that has been specially design and optimized to run virtual machines. Think of it as a mini-OS with drivers to talk to hardware components like network cards, storage devices, etc. And since it is from the virtual solution provider, it is truly both an effective and optimal solution. But that comfort zone comes with a cost (i.e. $$$).

Now look again at Figure 2.1 and notice that the freeware server product is essentially the exact same solution where the hypervisor is the client's operating system install. So, if the OS is paired down to its barest minimum, with the least overhead and excess of features enabled, the result would be the hypervisor. It may not be as efficient or nimble as the excellent hypervisor available from VMware, but it is both doable and 100% free. Moreover, upgrading from a personal OS to their hypervisor solution can be done anytime.

Performance Ramifications

The obvious question or bone of contention between these two key alternatives is performance. And yes, the vendor provided hypervisor is probably always going to be faster choice. This topic will be more thoroughly examined with empirical benchmark results in Chapter 8.

The question really becomes one of total cost. If one has Windows or Linux system administrators who already know how to configure the database server hardware routinely used, if one already has or knows where to go for drivers and updates, and if one is just more comfortable with not introducing yet another new technology to embrace, then the cost savings on the staffing alone could radically outstrip the meager savings on the software. Also, VMware permits one to move up as business requirements demand, so what is there to lose?

Besides, the recent trend of substantial and growing hardware performance improvements, which also happens to be why DBAs are now doing so much virtualization, means that reasonable overhead is now quite acceptable. Also, the bar to clear for being considered reasonable is lowering almost daily.

For example, a single database server from just five to six years ago costs four to five times as much as a server today – and today's servers come with multiple multi-core CPUs and lots of memory. So a 10-20% overhead is not that big of a deal anymore on a machine that has so much raw capacity that will be virtualized into multiple machines. Today's hardware is just too inexpensive and fast to make this the sole decision criteria anymore. These are truly great and interesting times.

An analogy might help here. Back in the 1970's oil crunch, automobiles got much worse fuel mileage and air conditioners were often an afterthought in terms of the car's overall engineering, i.e. efficiency. So driving with the AC on was doubly expensive. But today's cars get much better gas mileage and the air conditioners now have been engineered from the ground up as a key component of the vehicle. Hence, even though oil is nearing $100 per barrel, drivers don't consider driving with the AC off like back in the 1970's to save a few percentage points. Today, comfort is valued more and the cost is by far much less. In short, overhead is ignored because it is no longer relevant.

That is really not as cavalier an attitude as it may seem. Person hours cost so much more now than computer hardware even with inexpensive offshore outsourcing. It is now considered a sound business decision these days to throw cheap hardware at problems. It is at least, if not more, cost effective than having the staff tuned and optimized for the same net effect.

Besides, a failed tuning and optimization effort leaves you exactly where you started. At least the hardware upgrade approach results in a faster/better server experiencing the same problem that may still have future value to the business once the fundamental problem is eventually corrected. And if nothing else, the hardware can be depreciated, whereas the time spent tuning is always just a cost taken off the bottom line. So, with such cheap hardware, it might be a wiser business bet to throw hardware at some solutions sooner than was done in the past. One might go so far as to make an economic principle claim that the opportunity cost of tuning is foregoing cheap upgrades that might fix the issue and also possess intrinsic value. Stated this way, it is a safe bet that is where the business people would vote to spend.

The only reason this hardware-first attitude is being stressed is that, in the virtualized server world, it is generally best to think of hardware resources as just assets that are deployed when and where they are needed as they are needed. Also, a viable business solution is simply to deploy more assets as needed. Since the concept of the server (the asset) is now virtualized, it could well mean just assigning more CPUs or memory from a virtual pool to a particular virtual machine. In the virtual world, it is no longer necessary to think in terms of the physical constraints of a particular server, one must also think abstractly – which leads nicely into the next topic.

Ever Increasing Abstraction

One of the first and most obvious concessions a DBA makes in a virtualized server world is that there is yet another layer of hardware and software abstraction being forced into the overall equation. That latest injection of virtualization is pervasive now throughout all the hardware and software levels. The entire technology stack is very quickly becoming less and less concrete in day to day terms. Gone are the good old days of being able to walk into a server room and point to hardware. Also gone are the days of sizing totally independent of all other systems (remember, everything is becoming shared assets). These days, planning for minimum resource needs is based upon maintaining certain SLA levels, but it is no longer necessary to make the one-to-one correspondence between our needs and a single server. Instead, those needs should be expressed clearly enough so that someone can meet those requirements while deploying the database within their asset pool.

But fear not, for DBAs have embraced abstraction for years, even if they have forgotten about this fact. For example, as disk drives became bigger and file systems could support ever larger files, the logical volume manager appeared as an abstraction technique to simplify storage management. So DBAs evolved in their database storage thinking and planning as solutions built upon the foundations shown below by Figure 2.2.

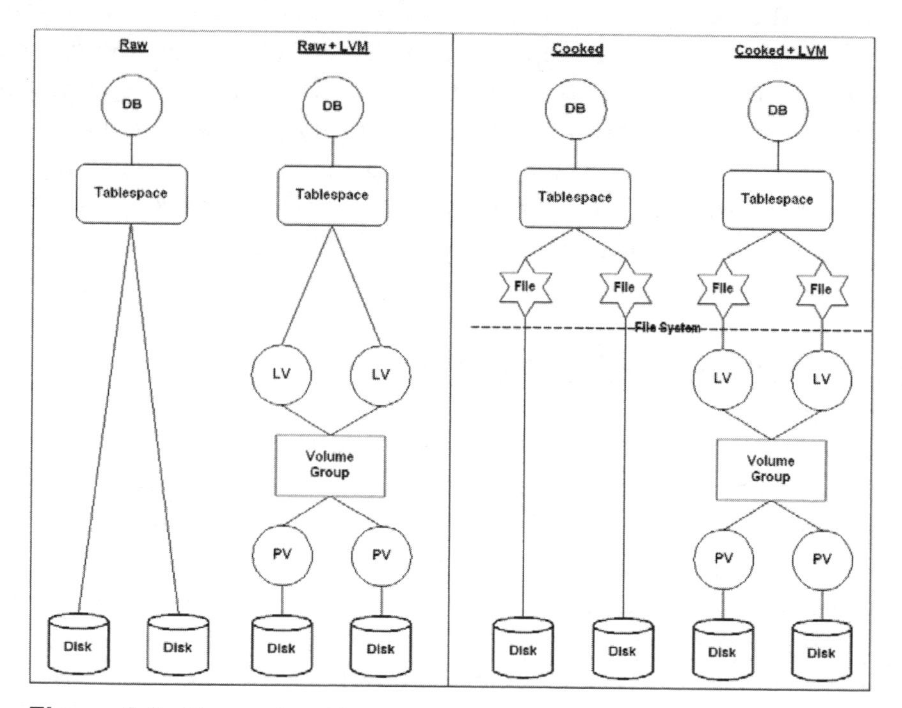

Figure 2.2: *Examples of Database Storage*

Before Logical Volume Managers (LVMs), storage space was assigned to tablespace data files as either raw disks or cooked files. Of course, one could also argue that the file system was actually the first abstraction. Then came LVMs, and now space can be managed one additional level removed. Add to that disk storage arrays where logical units or LUNs are allocated and assigned, and there is yet another level of abstraction.

Then along came 9i's Oracle Managed Files (OMF) and 10g's Automated Storage Management (shown in Figure 2.3). Now there are even more levels and types of storage abstraction. Since such abstraction often and generally made the DBA's life easier, these new techniques were embraced with minimal skepticism. Oracle even claimed, at the 11g new features training in Dallas in 2007, that SAME or stripe and mirror everything was more pervasive than ever before and a totally acceptable practice. In fact, they recommended fewer tablespaces and data files, thereby leaving the details buried in the abstraction. This author happens to agree. This author now separates tablespaces purely due to logical needs, such as different performance characteristics by which to categorize.

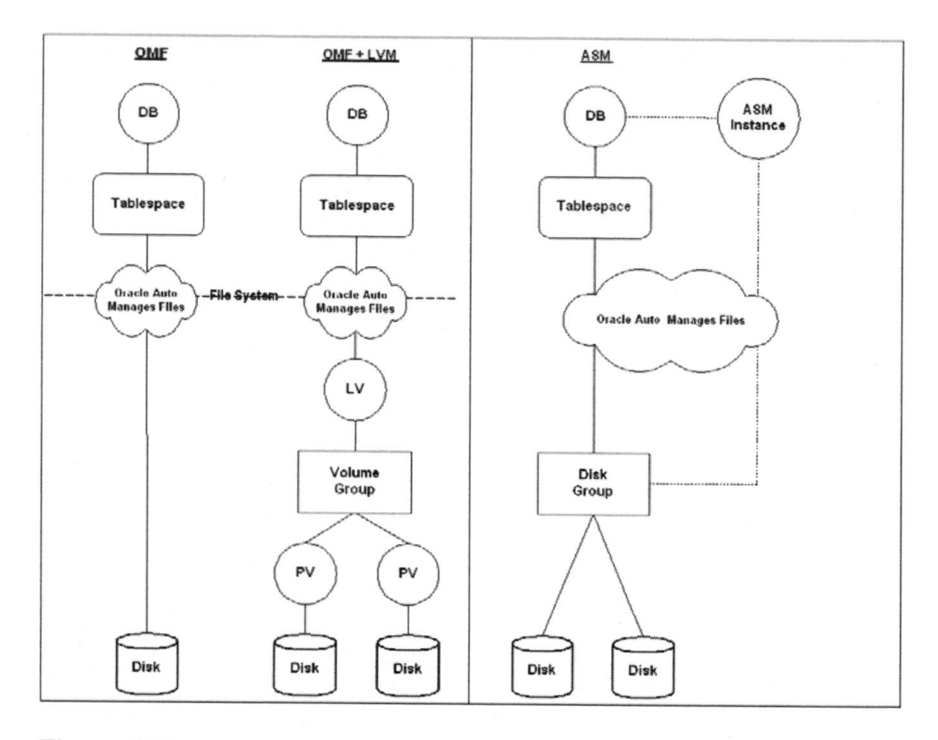

Figure 2.3: *Examples of Storage Abstraction – OMF and ASM*

The point is simply that DBAs have been accepting and doing abstraction for years, even if they forgot or failed to realize it. In fact, the adoption of ASM has been optimistically quoted as 65% of new RAC deployments and 25% of new non-RAC databases. This is not hard to believe since ASM makes space management so much easier.

Plus, with all the abstractions listed above, even more are happening in addition to server virtualization of which the DBA may or may not be aware. For example, with storage virtualization shown in the example in Figure 2.4, disk space may be assigned on high speed SCSI drives contained in a fiber channel connected SAN array, some space on a 10-gigabit NAS array, and some space on a 10-gigabit connected iSCSI array. Furthermore, the NAS and iSCSI arrays may contain a mixture of high speed SCSI disks, high speed IDE disks, and even possibly, some slower speed IDE disks. When a DBA asks for a few terabytes of disk space, they tend not to need to know the details and performance characteristics of every component in the stack as long as they meet their SLAs.

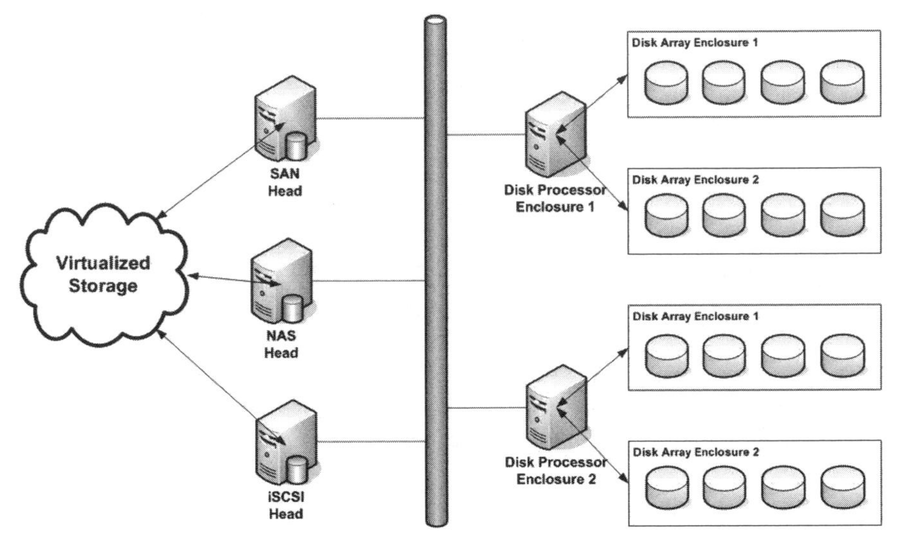

Figure 2.4: *Distribution of Virtualized Storage*

Therefore, server virtualization is just another in an ongoing series of abstractions being introduced throughout the technology stack. DBAs must become accustomed to and embrace virtualization, because the trend is clear – it is happening everywhere

Virtualized Oracle Architecture

So what does all this virtualization mean to the standard perception of the Oracle database architecture as shown in Figure 2.5?

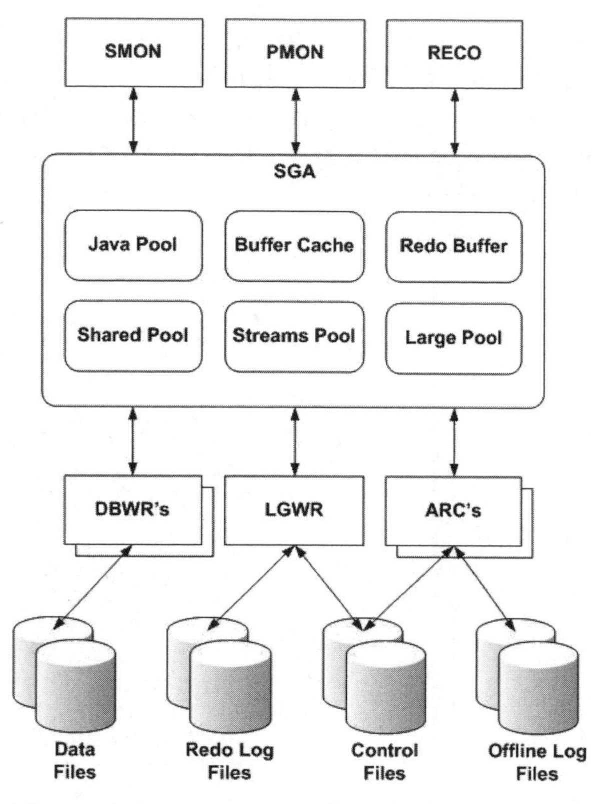

Figure 2.5: *Oracle Database Architecture*

Go back to the most fundamental definition of the term database: the Oracle processes, memory, and files. Now zoom out and the picture becomes just four fundamental components: shared memory, processes that are stand alone, processes that access files or devices, and files or devices. (Figure 2.6)

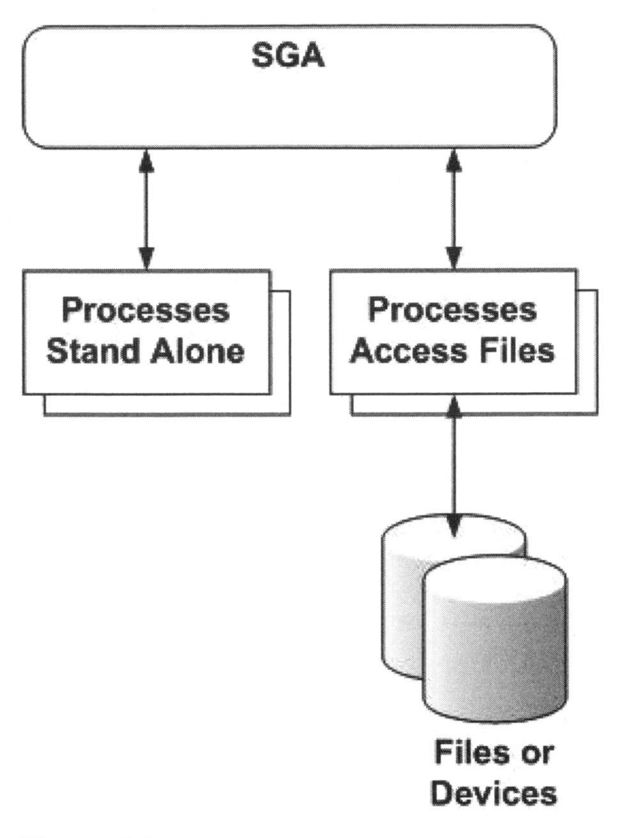

Figure 2.6: *Database Components*

Now combine the full-virtualization server depicted on the right side of Figure 2.1, Oracle ASM database instance depicted on the right side of Figure 2.3, virtualized storage shown in Figure 2.4, and the high-level Oracle architecture shown in Figure 2.6 to form the overall Oracle architecture in a virtualized world as shown below in Figure 2.7. This will also serve as the primary example throughout the rest of this book of deploying Oracle on a virtual server. Remember – this way it is free and can always be scaled up.

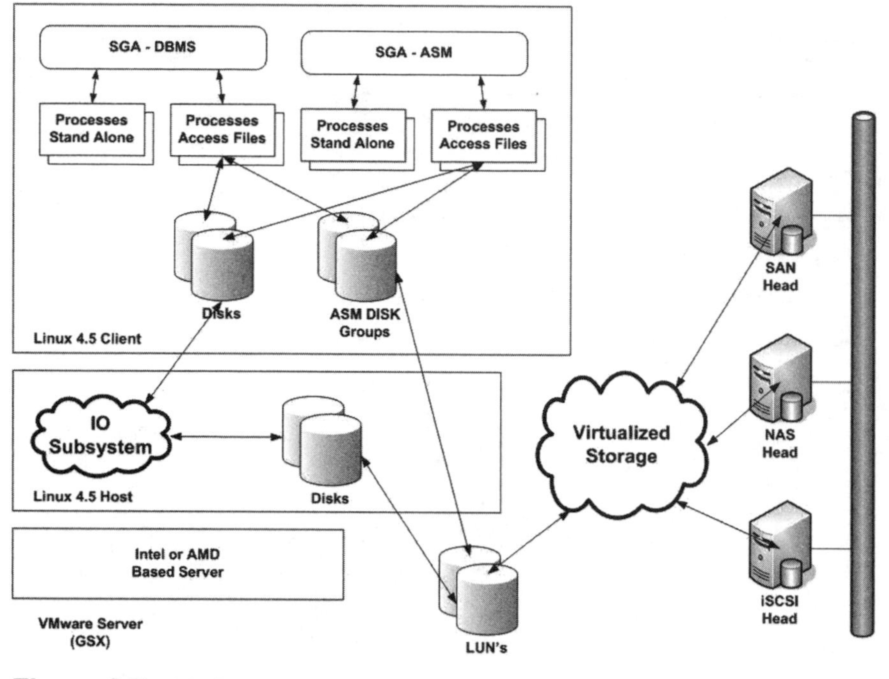

Figure 2.7: *Full Virtualization*

That is certainly of a lot of moving parts! If that is not bad enough, then think of how the picture would change with RAC. The one concept that this picture should clearly communicate is that in the virtualized world, nothing maps one-to-one anymore. So do not assume too much, especially as it relates to the assignment of the underlying hardware assets.

So why spend so much time correctly visualizing the overall architecture shown in Figure 2.7? The reason is because it is hard to optimize or tune that which cannot be comprehended. For example, in the old days, DBAs might have looked for disk hot-spots as part of their standard tuning regimen. But look again at Figure 2.7 and one really cannot point to the spindles anymore because they are multiple levels of abstraction removed. In fact, most database and operating system monitoring tools cannot see behind this veil of abstraction. So how would one look for a hot disk and should one even try?

The point is that database tuning and optimization cannot be approached in the same manner as in the past. Not only can the resources allocated dynamically change over time; but furthermore, the actual resources being allocated cannot be seen when they are static. This picture makes it very clear that tuning must be done differently. This topic will be covered in more detail in Chapter 9. In order to grasp and affect those new tuning/optimization techniques, performance metrics must be measured and questioned with the complete virtualized picture in mind. Otherwise, much like a confused dog, one could be perpetually chasing one's tail.

Lastly, none of these issues means that an Oracle database on a virtualized server cannot be effectively tuned. This just means it should be tuned smarter with current and future asset allocation always in mind.

Additional Complexities

This is not the end. If all these levels of increased abstraction were not enough, there is yet another wrinkle to this new and overly complex environment in which DBAs must now function. With the specialization and/or segregation of job responsibilities typical in many enterprise information systems areas these days, a DBA might have to talk to three or more people to implement a database within such a virtualized environment as shown in Figure 2.7. So a DBA might have to talk to people whose various roles and/or titles might include:

- Storage Administrator
- Network Administrator
- Operating System Administrator

- Virtualization Asset Administrator
- Infrastructure Architecture Consultant

And as is commonly known, the lines of communication grow exponentially based on the number of people one has to work with to get a job done. The communication complexity formula most often quoted is:

$$\text{Lines of Communication} = N * (N - 1) / 2$$

Thus, the DBA has some 30 distinct lines of communication with just the few additional people listed above. That means more email, more phone calls, longer meetings, less agreement, and often, longer times until a consensus is reached. So the DBA's job is made that much more difficult, especially when good DBAs tend to be heads down technical experts who would rather just do the work than sit around and talk about it.

Conclusion

Examined in this chapter, within the virtualization universe, were the architectural alternatives that clearly appear as reasonable choices, the performance ramifications of such choices, the ever increasing amount of abstraction DBAs must accept and embrace, and finally, the resulting Oracle database architecture within all these contexts. The reason for this explanation and analysis was that today's DBA cannot reliably operate upon a virtualized database for many tasks, such as tuning and optimization, unless they can do so comfortably within the confines of their very complex hardware and political environment. But once armed with the proper fundamental architectural information revealed here, the DBA should be in good position for all the topics yet to be covered in this book.

Host Setup

When Oracle performance suffers, the DBA is blamed first!

Host Impacts

How true the above cartoon rings since every DBA feels like they are wearing such a target. Furthermore, many DBAs feel like all those who are shooting arrows have the rapid-fire crossbow from the 2004 "Van Helsing" movie. Because when the "fecal matter hits the fan," the DBA stands at the forefront and foremost against the ensuing onslaught. At times like that, just remember DBAs chose this profession.

But the above cartoon rings true for another reason in the virtualized world; namely, the onion-like nature of the abstracted technology layers upon which databases have been built. The center ring (i.e. the one with the highest point value) is the virtual host, and the most valuable tuning and optimization goals can be achieved by maximizing the raw performance of that host. The mantra in the virtualized world is that any database server guest can be no more optimized than the host containing it, so always make sure to get the host right from the start.

Also, remember that optimizations made to the host will apply to multiple database guests, so twice the benefits can be realized. Often, fixing a host performance problem whose symptoms are realized by optimizing that host for just a single guest can translate into improved performance for most, if not all, the guests running on that host. All of that can be accomplished for the singular cost of finding and tuning that one issue centrally.

Furthermore, highly shared hosts (i.e. those with the more guests) will realize cumulative magnified improvements and thus, triple-dipping in terms of benefits. For example, a host with four database servers is having some performance issues. By tuning the host using one database guest as the test subject, the DBA finds that a host change can provide a 10% improvement. However, once that host is running all four of its guests once again, the observed improvement is magnified by the fact that the benefits are realized globally and concurrently. So, in effect, that single 10% may translate into much more than 10% net.

Hardware Considerations

This may seem like an extraneous section to include, but this author has seen quite a few people running virtual machines in non-conducive hardware setups and then wrongly thinking virtualization was not up to snuff. The obvious realities are that the hardware must be sufficient to handle one or more database servers, their operating systems, plus the host operating system to boot. So it should come as no surprise that having as much CPU and memory as budget will allow is highly recommended. That is good advice if new hardware is being ordered, but what about reusing existing hardware assets or laptops/notebooks for demos?

When trying to utilize existing hardware, just remember that if the server was not good enough for application X, then it probably will not be sufficient for X + Y or even Y + Z, unless both are much smaller than X. Basically it boils down to one simple rule: if a server was not sufficient for a stand-alone situation, then reusing it as a virtualized server is most likely an exercise in futility. Hardware is so inexpensive these days that one should buy what is needed. Remember, person hours to tune a system will very often cost more than a server these days, so overspending on hardware is a good investment.

Possibly the most egregious situation encounter is people trying to improve sub-standard virtualization hardware via system component augmentations that are in and of themselves neither a true nor good performance option. For example, many people will try to run VMware on their notebooks for an Oracle database contained on a USB disk drive. The USB interface has 2.5-3.0 times slower throughput than SCSI or IDE channels are capable of, so this is a very poor choice. It would be much better to simply buy a replacement disk for the laptop/notebook.

For example, upgrading a notebook from 100GB to 200GB costs $150 and two hours to move the image from the source to the target drive. Even if the imaging software has been purchased for just that one use, the cost would have been just another $50, for a total of $200. Since even the cheapest people charge at least $50 per hour for their time, the true upgrade cost was approximately

$300 ($150 for new disk drive, $50 for imaging software, and $100 for two hours time). This can be nearly guaranteed to improve performance by at least a factor of two. Whereas, it cannot be said with any certainty that six hours of tuning, which would equate to $300 @ $50 per hour, will yield similarly positive results.

Another pandemic problem that is often encountered is someone trying to use cheap IDE disk drives on virtualized servers. Even the fastest SATA-II IDE drives are not as fast as SCSI or SAS (Serial Attached SCSI). SCSI drives spin much faster, often from 10-15,000 RPM versus just 5,400 to 7,200 for IDE. Although Western Digital makes Raptor IDE drives which spin at 10,000 RPM, they are both expensive and relatively uncommon. So this rotational speed difference alone can translate into as much as a 100% improvement.

Furthermore, IDE disk drives have another huge disadvantage – they primarily perform I/O operations serially, in that they complete I/O operation #1 before doing I/O operation #2. Even SATA IDE drives that support Native Command Queuing (NCQ) or Tagged Command Queuing (TCQ), which permit the disk to reorder I/O requests to minimize head movement, still perform their I/O operations serially. Whereas, SCSI drives possess a processor to minimize host CPU usage and permit higher throughput of concurrent I/O requests. Also, since a virtualized server is going to need all of its CPU resources and needs to be able to handle lots of concurrent I/Os from multiple operating systems, SCSI based technology is clearly the best choice.

Regardless of whether a new virtual server is being ordered or an existing box's bandwidth is simply being augmented to support running multiple virtual machines and their databases, it is important to choose an I/O channel that can support such high

I/O loads across multiple shared resources. And stated previously, IDE is not a good answer – SCSI reigns supreme. But what kind of SCSI based technology should be implemented? Again, much of that depends upon the hardware budget. Assuming a minimal budget required for a proper I/O subsystem, some good choices include:

- For Direct Attached Storage (DAS) – with multiple controllers
    - SCSI-320
    - SAS (Serial Attached SCSI)
    - SCSI-640
- For Storage Area Networks (SAN) – with multiple HBA's (host bus adapters), directors/channels, & redundant pathways
    - Fibre Channel 1GFC
    - iSCSI via 1Gb Ethernet
    - Fibre Channel 2GFC
    - Fibre Channel 4GFC
    - iSCSI via 10Gb Ethernet

The entire universe of I/O subsystem choices are shown in the table on the following page with all the above stated good choices highlighted.

INTERFACE	THROUGHPUT (MB / SEC)
PATA PIO Mode 0	3
SCSI-1	5
PATA PIO Mode 1	5.2
PATA PIO Mode 2	8.3
Fast SCSI 2	10

INTERFACE	THROUGHPUT (MB / SEC)
PATA PIO Mode 3	11.1
iSCSI / 100Mb Ethernet	12.5
PATA PIO Mode 4	16.7
Fast-Wide SCSI 2	20
Ultra SCSI	20
Ultra DMA PATA 33	33
Ultra Wide SCSI	40
Ultra2 SCSI	40
USB 2.0	60
Ultra2 Wide SCSI	80
Ultra DMA PATA 66	66
Ultra DMA PATA 100	100
Fibre Channel 1GFC	106.26
iSCSI / 1Gb Ethernet	125
Ultra DMA PATA 133	133
SATA 150	150
Ultra3 SCSI-160	160
Fibre Channel 2GFC	212.5
SATA 300	300
eSATA	300
Ultra-320 SCSI	320
SAS 1	375
Fibre Channel 4GFC	425
SATA 600 (not yet)	600
Ultra-640 SCSI	640
SAS 2 (not yet)	750
Fibre Channel 8GFC	850
iSCSI / 10Gb Ethernet	1250

Table 3.1: *I/O subsystem choices*

Therefore, it is very important that one have the proper virtualization hardware and be financially able to create an I/O subsystem to fit ones needs. To use anything less is to create more headaches and aggravation that could be easily avoided with the right equipment.

BIOS Basics

There is one very critical and universal hardware recommendation this author makes to anyone deploying database servers, whether virtualized or not, and that is to not enable Hyper-Threading on your server's CPUs. Never do this no matter how much the urge to double the processor count may be. These are really not true CPUs, but rather a technique by which to trick the operating system into thinking there are twice as many processors. Database benchmarks show that the performance penalty has always been around 20%. The reason is simple; database operations tend to cause a stall and flush of the CPU instruction cache by their I/O intensive nature. Such stalls are the most expensive (i.e. worst) thing for Hyper-Threaded CPUs to process. So avoid it at all costs on all of database servers!

Not every motherboard and BIOS offers the same settings to tweak or otherwise optimize the server's performance. Listed below are some guidelines for things to consider possibly setting via the BIOS depending on the specific business requirements or special technical needs:

- Virtualization Technology = ENABLED
- Virus warning = DISABLED
- CPU level 1 cache = ENABLED
- CPU level 2 cache = ENABLED
- APIC mode = ENABLED
- Hyper-Threading = DISABLED

- HDD S.M.A.R.T. capability = DISABLED
- FSB spread spectrum = DISABLED
- AGP spread spectrum = DISABLED
- System BIOS cacheable = DISABLED
    - Video BIOS cacheable = DISABLED
    - Video BIOS shadowing = DISABLED
    - Video RAM cacheable = DISABLED
    - On board audio = DISABLED
    - On board modem = DISABLED
    - On board 1394 (Firewire) = DISABLED
    - On board serial ports = DISABLED
    - On board parallel ports = DISABLED
    - On board game ports = DISABLED
    - ACPI suspend to RAM = DISABLED
    - PCI/VGA Palette Snoop = DISABLED

Remember, the goal is to configure a machine to function as a server, and a virtual server at that. So it is very unlikely that anything besides the CPU, memory, I/O and network bandwidths will be needed. Therefore, many BIOS settings can be disabled. This can improve performance and save power, which are both desirable. Furthermore, some of the above recommended values will also result in a more stable system.

Host OS Selection

Sometimes this critical decision has already been made. For example, if working in an all Windows or all Linux shop, the choice is clear and simple. Or if setting up a laptop/notebook for doing demos and Windows is still the predominate operating system in general business use. So again, the choice may well have been already been made. Regardless, the steps that follow will pretty much remain the same.

Sometimes other options or alternative exist when selecting the host's operating system, and that too takes just a little thought. When only going to virtualization software (i.e. the hypervisor), the host operating system selection is of little importance. Thus, a simple rule can be used here: what is inexpensive, light-weight and relatively stable?

The answer is Linux. It is free, can take as little as a few hundred megabytes to install and run, and offers quite good reliability these days. Plus, it is easy to streamline down to a very bare, high speed installation. Not to mention that working with it is fun!

Now, it is not this author's intent to start a heated political debate or religious war here. The host OS simply serves one purpose and that is being a container to run the hypervisor and clients. The clients then can use whatever operating system under which the application or database works best. So why spend money to purchase a host operating system?

Of course, some system administrators and database administrators may still have a few reservations about Linux and its maturity and/or acceptance. IDC had projected that Linux would be mainstream long before now, even within the mission critical enterprise applications and database space as shown in Figure 3.1. [Linux: A Journey into the Enterprise, IDC, 2001]

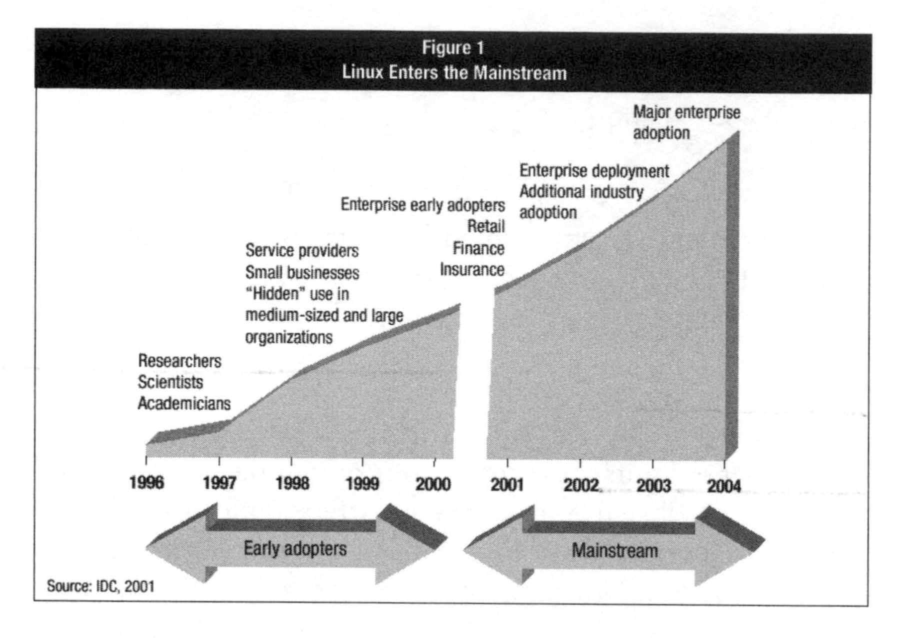

Figure 3.1: *Linux Enters the Mainstream*

Furthermore, Gartner has tracked Linux adoption progress and shown that while it has not been quite as optimistic as projected, it is still well within reach of being considered mainstream by the end of 2007 (see Figure 2). [Linux Marches Toward Mainstream Adoption, Gartner, Scott & Weiss, 2003]

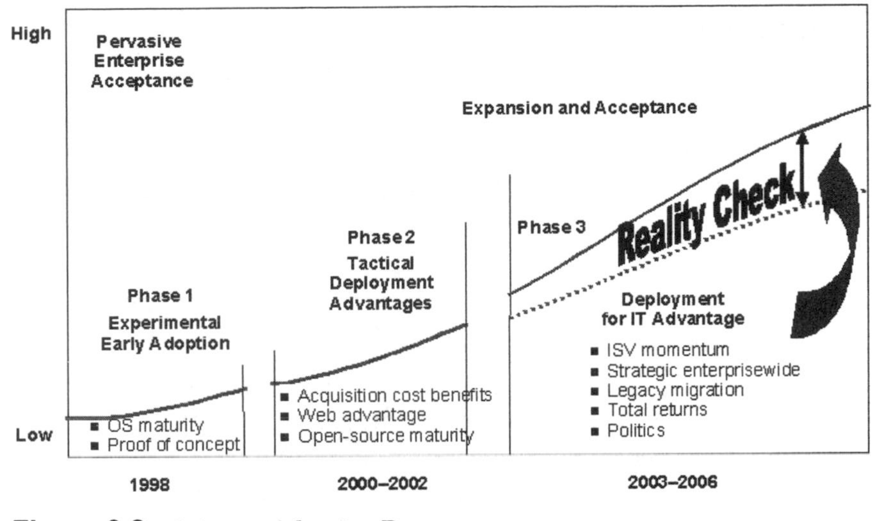

Figure 3.2: *Linux Adoption Progress*

This is not to say that Linux is either superior or preferred. It simply begs the question, why pay for Windows as the virtual host operating system when that host is only needed to run the hypervisor in order to run the virtual clients?

The next logical question might be which distribution to choose. Remember that the primary objective is to create a host to run the virtual clients, which then run Oracle. Thus, it is not necessary to pick one of the Linux distributions supported by Oracle for running their database (i.e. Red Hat, SuSE, Enterprise Linux, etc). Yet common sense would dictate standardizing on a single distribution to keep overall maintenance costs lower.

And, finally, for those who still prefer Microsoft Windows, just be sure to pick a server version of their operating system products such as Windows 2000 Server or Windows 2003 Server (and preferably 64-bit).

Host OS Install

The goal here is to create a minimal and streamlined host operating system environment to serve as the virtualized server. In essence, create a hypervisor based paravirtualization solution, so the host operating system needs to be very slim and trim. Therefore, it may be prudent to navigate the host operating system install looking for excesses to eliminate. Keep in mind that this machine is not going to be used like a regular server, desktop or laptop; instead, the minimum necessary to run the virtual machine clients is all that is necessary. That is exactly what Oracle did when they made the Oracle VM server. It is just a minimalist Linux kernel with support for a broad array of devices, file systems, software RAID volume management, and a special hypervisor to manage virtual server clients.

The prior section's BIOS settings to disable many features may also result in certain operating system components either not installing or not loading on boot. Either way, the end result is a much faster host operating system environment. However, do not just assume that turning off the BIOS will always achieve the desired results. During the operating system install, make sure to choose to leave off any additional hardware components or features that the virtual server will not need. This includes support for hardware such as the following:

- Modem
- Printer
- Firewire
- Infrared
- Speakers
- Microphones
- USB ports (if not needed for keyboard, mouse or flash disks)

Also, during the host operating system install, it will be beneficial to choose not to install many software features, options, or their support. For example, none of the following software components are truly necessary for a virtualized server's host operating system in order for it to effectively and efficiently house the virtual clients:

- Firewalls
- Extended Security (i.e. SE Linux)
- Office/Productivity
- Email Clients
- Email Servers
- Fax Support
- Graphics
- Sound & Video
- Instant Messengers
- DNS Servers
- Network Servers
- Web Servers
- Database Servers
- File Sharing
- File Indexing

Once the minimal host operating system has been successfully installed, the next step is to disable any and all unnecessary services or background processes such as the following:

Linux:

- anacron
- apmd

- atd
- autofs
- cups
- cupsconfig
- gpm
- isdn
- iptables
- kudzu
- netfs
- nfslock
- pcmcia
- portmap
- rhnsd
- sendmail

Windows:

- Alerter
- Automatic Updates
- Clip Book
- Error Reporting
- Help & Support
- Indexing
- Messenger
- NetMeeting Remote Desktop Sharing
- Remote Desktop Help Session Manager
- System Restore Service

- Task Scheduler
- TCP/IP NetBIOS Helper
- Telephony
- Terminal Services
- Themes

The end result should be an effective and efficient base operating system that is now conducive for hosting virtual clients, which will be covered more in the next chapter. To eek every last drop of performance from the host, further optimization can be performed. As stated previously, the mantra in the virtualized world is that any database server guest can be no more optimized than the host containing it, so always make sure to get the host right from the start.

Incremental Host Tuning

The next step is to tune the host operating system both for virtualization and concurrent database oriented client workloads. It is really no different than tuning a stand-alone database server except that the host is one step or level of abstraction removed. Simply make sure to minimize any unnecessary overhead and, thus, maximize the overall performance. The only difference is that CPU, memory, and I/O assumptions need to be made a lot more generically since the hardware will be shared across hosted clients. So, optimally, all tuning efforts should apply relatively well across hosted clients, therefore realizing the double-dipping and triple-dipping effects stated earlier.

The chief new complexity is that the DBA now may have multiple databases using some shared resources, much like historically hosting multiple databases on a single box, and thus, need to account for that at some point during tuning. But each optimization step should occur in its own due time. Tune the virtual server host first. Then tune each of the virtual machines clients, which will be covered in the next chapter, as though still implementing single database per server deployments, which technically speaking, could occur at some point even in a virtual world. And finally, tune the host operating system for side effects caused by sharing resources, but do not start here or try to do it all in one pass.

Much like any scientific experiment or database benchmarking only a single variable per test iteration should be changed so that its results can be properly measured and observed. This technique is called "Incremental Tuning" it should be considered both the mandatory and only reliable way to correctly optimize any computer system, especially a virtualized host running multiple virtual clients.

Optimize by Subsystem

It is best to think of a virtual host server as being composed of four basic subsystems, which should be the focus of any OS tuning efforts:

- CPU
- Memory
- I/O
- Network

Furthermore, all the above areas should be tuned with the server's purpose in mind – hosting multiple virtual clients. The basic idea being that the overall performance can be no better or worse than the sum of its parts. Additionally, all of the above are possibly dynamic in the virtual world, so again making more generic assumptions should generally lead to better aggregate results. This is really nothing more than Incremental Tuning applied at the first granular level of interest: the subsystems.

We will now look at doing just this for both Linux and Windows. Note that all these techniques would apply in some fashion to other operating systems such as Sun Solaris, Hewlett Packard's HP-UX or IBM's AIX. In all cases, it is assumed that simply installing a clean basic host operating system is something the user finds both comfortable and familiar. A summarization is included at the end of the chapter as well for future quick reference.

Optimizing Linux

With today's cheap hardware costs, it is safe to assume a virtual server host will have multiple processors and lots of memory, most likely greater than 4 GB. And since the virtual server host is the relative center of the universe so to speak, it therefore cannot offer up to clients anything which it cannot itself do or access. So go with 64-bit Linux unless there is some hardware driver issue that prevents this choice.

There is one more little tweak that should be applied to any 64-bit Linux server with significant memory and that is the use of huge pages. This Linux 2.6 kernel feature simply utilizes larger than the 4K pages to reduce virtual memory I/O operations when working with lots of memory. Here are some documented limits:

HARDWARE PLATFORM	KERNEL 2.4	KERNEL 2.6
Linux x86 (IA32)	4MB	4MB
Linux x86-64 (AMD64, EM64T)	2MB	2MB
Linux Itanium (IA64)	256MB	256MB
IBM Power Based Linux (PPC64)	NA	16MB
IBM zSeries Based Linux	NA	NA
IBM S/390 Based Linux	NA	NA

Table 3.2: *Linux limits*

The process to enable huge pages is as follows:

- X = grep Hugepagesize /proc/meminfo
- Y = Largest (MB of all client SGA's) * 1024
- Z = # Huge Pages needed = Y / X
- Set Huge Page Pool size
  - edit /etc/sysctl.conf
  - vm.nr_hugepages = Z
- Increase ulimit parameter *memlock* for oracle user
  - edit /etc/security/limits.conf
  - oracle soft memlock Y
  - oracle hard memlock Y
- reboot

To improve I/O for file system requests made by the hosted clients and/or their databases, Linux offers a little known and seldom used option that can yield between 50-150% performance improvements in standard database benchmarks like the TPC-C by simply changing the /etc/fstab file entries for the Oracle data file mount points as follows:

- For ext2 and 3 file systems, add ",noatime" to the third column.

What this does is tell the operating system that it is not necessary to update the *last access time* for directories and files under that mount point, which translates into radically reduced total I/O. Since the host file system is simply a mechanism to provide abstracted storage to its clients, why spend I/O resources to update time attributes for files or directories? Especially when it is fairly unlikely they will ever be accessed for any reason other than maybe doing backups.

The one last item to consider for optimizing Linux on a virtual server host is to compile a monolithic kernel, which is nothing more than the kernel compiled to only load those must-have features and not load those that are unnecessary. However, in order to not goof up the Linux install, the DBA better be comfortable with compiling, linking, and installing a new kernel. (Not really, but just be very sure before going this route!) It consists of the following rather easy steps:

- cd /usr/src/linux or /usr/src/kernels/xxx where xxx is the kernel source version
- make mrproper (simply cleans up under that directory tree)
- make config or xconfig (if Linux install supports X-Windows)
- answer all the questions on what to compile or load into the resulting kernel and what not to – thus reducing its size, memory footprint and complexity
- make dep; make clean; make bzImage
- cp/usr/src/linux/arch/i386/boot/bzImage/vmlinuz-kernel.version.number
- cp/src/linux/System.map/boot/System.map-kernel.version.number

- edit/boot/grub/grub.conf
  - have image= point to new kernel version binaries

The only other item to consider for optimization is to recompile and relink the C runtime library with more optimistic compiler optimization directives. This step requires perfect execution since any failure along the way means a total reinstall of the Linux OS. Therefore, it is generally advisable that most people not attempt this step although it has been known to yield significant performance improvements for those who can successfully complete it.

Optimizing Windows

As with Linux, it is safe to assume a virtual server host will have multiple processors and lots of memory, most likely greater than 4 GB. Thus, it is best to go with 64-bit Windows server editions unless there is some hardware driver issue that prevents this choice.

While this author likes Windows 2000 Server as much as the next guy and feels that it is a great candidate for being the virtual server host operating system, it is nonetheless 7+ years old and getting a wee bit long in the tooth. Actually, the biggest problem is getting drivers for newer hardware on this platform. So Windows 2003 Server is really the only way to go and 64-bit Enterprise Edition Release 2 is the most highly recommended.

To improve I/O for file system based Oracle data files, Windows offers a little known and seldom used option that can yield between 50-150% performance improvements in standard database benchmarks like the TPC-C by simply changing the Windows registry setting as follows:

- HKEY_LOCAL_MACHINE\System\CurrentControlSet\Control\FileSystem\ NtfsDisableLastAccessUpdate=1

What this does is set the operating system to *disable last access update* for directories and files on this Windows server, which translates into radically reduced total I/O. Since the Oracle background processes are accessing the data files every 3 seconds and have their own headers with timestamps within them, why spend I/O resources to update time attributes for files or directories?

Some other common Windows registry tweaks for database servers include:

- Disable 8 dot 3 Name Creation - This setting controls the generation of MS-DOS compatible 8.3 file names on NTFS partitions. Disabling this feature can increase performance on high usage partitions that have a large amount of files with long filenames. Setting this option also toggles whether to permit extended characters to be used in 8.3 filenames.
- Enable a large size file system cache – This entry controls whether the system maintains a standard size or a large size file system cache. Enabling a larger cache makes sense for networked database servers with sufficient memory.
- Disable paging of the kernel code - This entry controls whether the user and kernel mode drivers and the kernel mode core system code itself can be paged. Disabling the paging of kernel code makes sense for database servers with sufficient memory.
- I/O Page Lock Limit - This entry controls the maximum amount of RAM that can be locked for I/O operations. The default minimizes RAM usage. An I/O intensive system could benefit from larger buffer sizes. Caution: setting this parameter too high can result in slower performance. Set it in increments and see how it affects the system.

The corresponding recommended registry settings are as follows:

- HKEY_LOCAL_MACHINE\System\CurrentControlSet\Control\FileSystem\NtfsDisable8dot3NameCreation = 1
- HKEY_LOCAL_MACHINE\System\CurrentControlSet\Control\FileSystem\NtfsAllowExtendedCharacterIn8dot3Name = 0
- HKEY_LOCAL_MACHINE\System\CurrentControlSet\Control\SessionManager\MemoryManagement\LargeSystemCache = 1
- HKEY_LOCAL_MACHINE\System\CurrentControlSet\Control\SessionManager\MemoryManagement\DisablePagingExecutive=1
- HKEY_LOCAL_MACHINE\System\CurrentControlSet\Control\SessionManager\MemoryManagement\
- IoPageLockLimit = N, where N is chosen as follows:
  - if RAM <= 32MB then
  - IoPageLockLimit = 512
  - if RAM > 32MB then
  - IoPageLockLimit = 4K
  - if RAM > 64MB then
  - IoPageLockLimit = 8K
  - if RAM > 128MB then
  - IoPageLockLimit = 16K
  - if RAM > 160MB then
  - IoPageLockLimit = 32K
  - if RAM > 256MB then
  - IoPageLockLimit = 64K

Included on the book's DVD and download website is a free Windows program to easily set all these parameters on both local and remote database server as shown below in Figure 3.

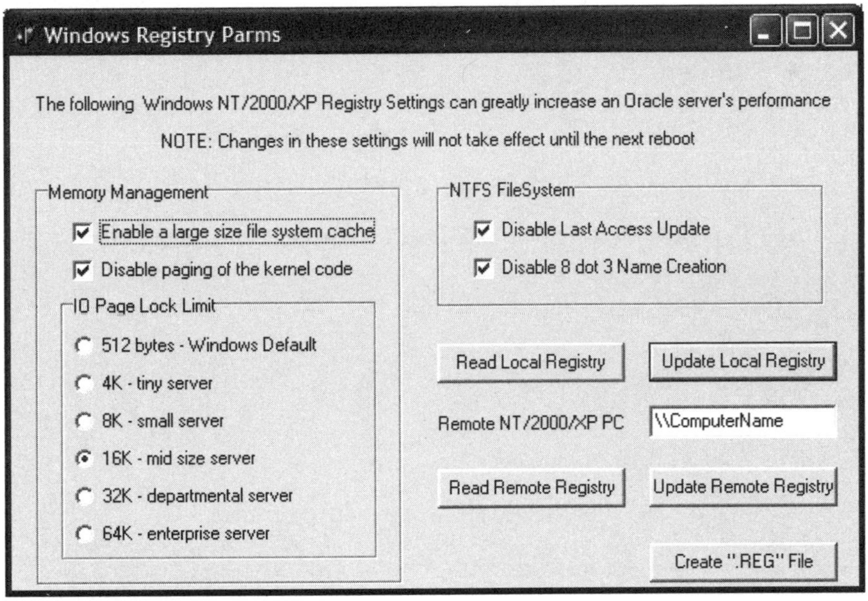

Figure 3.3: *Windows Registry Settings*

Obviously, installing anti-virus and anti-spyware software on the virtual server host is totally unnecessary because all it is going to do is run the operating system and hypervisor so that it can run clients. There will generally be very little direct use of this machine, except perhaps by the administrator during routine maintenance operations such as OS patches and backups.

Quick Reference

Below is a summary of the recommended host optimizations:

BIOS

- Disable Hyper-Threading

- Enable Virtualization Support

Linux:

- Kernel
  - 64-bit
  - SMP Support
  - Compile and link a "Monolithic" kernel
  - Possibly recompile/re-link C-runtime library
- Memory
  - Huge Pages
- I/O
  - /etc/fstab add *",noatime"*
- Remove non-essential software components
- Disable non-essential background processes/services

Windows:

- Version
- 64-bit
- Windows 2003 Enterprise R2
- Registry (use my freeware program to update)
- Disable last access update
- Disable 8 dot 3 name creation
  - Enable large size file system cache
  - Disable paging of kernel code
  - IO Page Lock Limit >= 16K
  - Remove non-essential software components

- Disable non-essential background processes/services
- No anti-virus or anti-spyware programs installed

Conclusion

This chapter explored how to best configure the centralized host and its subsystems in order to maximize database performance. The goal was to hit the center bulls-eye in order to score the most points, which meant to optimize the host first and foremost. All of these techniques should be considered as best practices and liberally implemented across all host machines for the benefit of all their guest operating systems. The cost to implement each of these concepts is relatively small, but both their individual and cumulative performance impacts are well worth the trouble.

Guest Setup

CHAPTER 4

Virtual Impacts

Assume that the Oracle database server is deployed on a VMware Guest operating system. If the database expected or required performance is sub par, what can be done? In other words – what does the above cartoon's "Move it to a faster server" solution really mean?

In the good old days of non-virtualized servers, databases were tuned and/or optimized at the server level itself because, in many cases, a database instance equated to a single non-shared server. One would simply spend X hours of effort to fix the performance problem and, hopefully as a final resort, reluctantly upgrade the server itself. But with today's extremely cheap hardware, it is almost more cost effective to jump straight to the hardware upgrades, sometimes even in a hapless shotgun approach to improve performance, since computers are now much cheaper than technical person hours – especially with today's relatively inexpensive offshore outsourcing!

This is further exasperated because in the virtual server world, one does not really have a physical box associated with the database. Instead, the database server is hosted on a virtual server, so there is at least one additional level of abstraction. In fact, with dynamic virtualization capabilities and products, some system administrators will simply be able to allocate more hardware resources to virtual machines from a centralized pool of excess capacity as they are needed. Furthermore, some modern virtualization products can increasingly do this automatically within some administrator defined business mandated service level agreement (SLA) thresholds.

Thus, the following choices exist as legitimate ways to improve database performance:

- Move the virtual machine to a larger host server
- Improve the hardware resources on the host server
- Move the virtual machine to a less utilized host server
- Move another virtual machine off that host server
- Allocate more virtual resources to that virtual machine
- De-allocate virtual resources from other virtual machines
- Increase that virtual machine's dynamic load balancing weight
- Switch from full virtualization to paravirtualization to better utilize the host's hardware resources (less host OS overhead)

The first two options are much like the choices of old. But look at all these new alternatives. And as time goes on, there will probably be more. In fact, who knows – maybe one day Oracle's

Grid Computing technology stack will equate to and, therefore, directly support the virtual machine as a key grid component. The future seems almost limitless.

Therefore, the "Move it to a faster server" solution really does not mean the same thing anymore. As with most things in life, it is now a wee bit more complicated. But that is okay because the DBA can just think of it as more job security!

Virtual Ramifications

The key concept to remember at all times while tuning a virtual machine is that either its underlying hardware resources or virtual hardware allocations may well change over time, usually to increase the capacity to meet increasing demands. So choices need to be made that will automatically scale forward. For once, it is possible to error on the side of optimism!

Assuming the virtual host server has been correctly optimized, then defining an appropriate virtual machine configuration and finally optimizing its guest operating system is the next logical step. The first part is relatively straightforward and the second part is really no different than tuning a stand-alone database server. Make sure to account for correctly setting configuration files, operating system parameters, and database parameters as always. The only difference is that CPU, memory, and I/O assumptions need to be made more generically since the true hardware has been abstracted and may change over time.

VM Creation

Think of the virtual machine (VM) as the planning-level hardware platform. Most DBAs would historically have had input or feedback on hardware platform selection and sometimes even worked with hardware vendors to properly size a machine for its intended database demands. Hence, DBAs should be interested in defining the VM configuration parameters because these settings will define the hardware universe within which the guest operating system will function. If a limit is posed at the VM settings level, there will be little to no operating system or database tuning which can compensate for these selections. It is that important, so do not skip or make light of this step!

So now the process of defining a VM and the options which have significant database performance ramifications will be examined. The first step to creating the VM is to specify what the guest operating system will be as shown below in Figure 4.1.

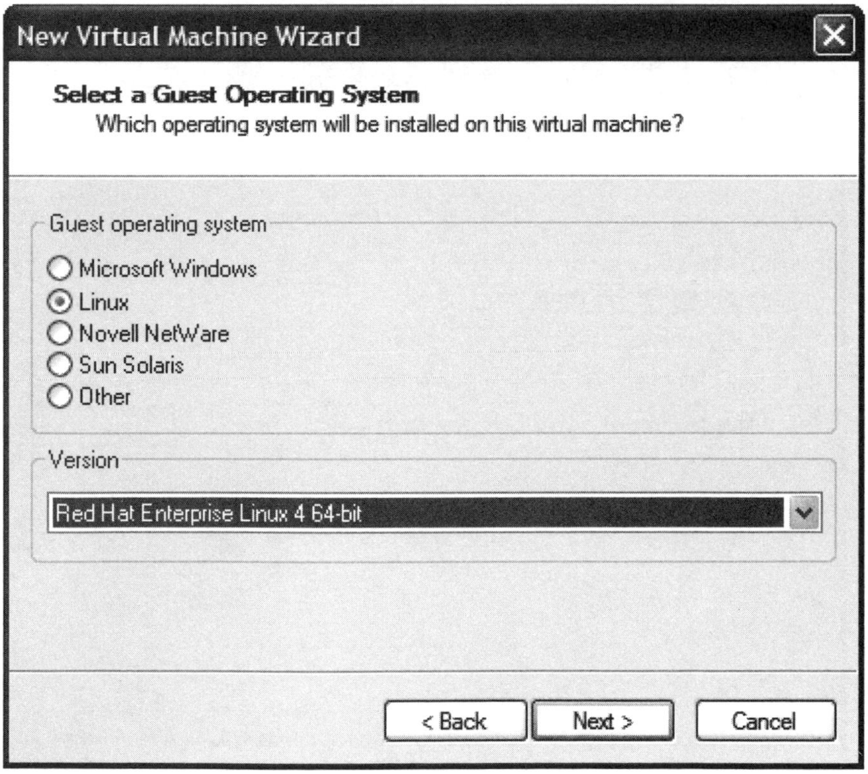

Figure 4.1: *Guest Operating System Choices*

This step seems fairly straightforward. But remember the mantra of erring on the side of optimism. Most servers' CPUs are 64-bits these days, so why be limited to 32-bits and its memory limitations? Unless a specific hardware or software incompatibility exists, go with 64-bit operating systems. This includes Windows 2003 Enterprise Edition R2 because there is an optimized version of the Oracle database for that specific platform.

The second step is also very simple and relatively straightforward. Specify the name and location of the virtual machine (i.e. its metadata and location of its base install for the OS). This step is shown below in Figure 4.2.

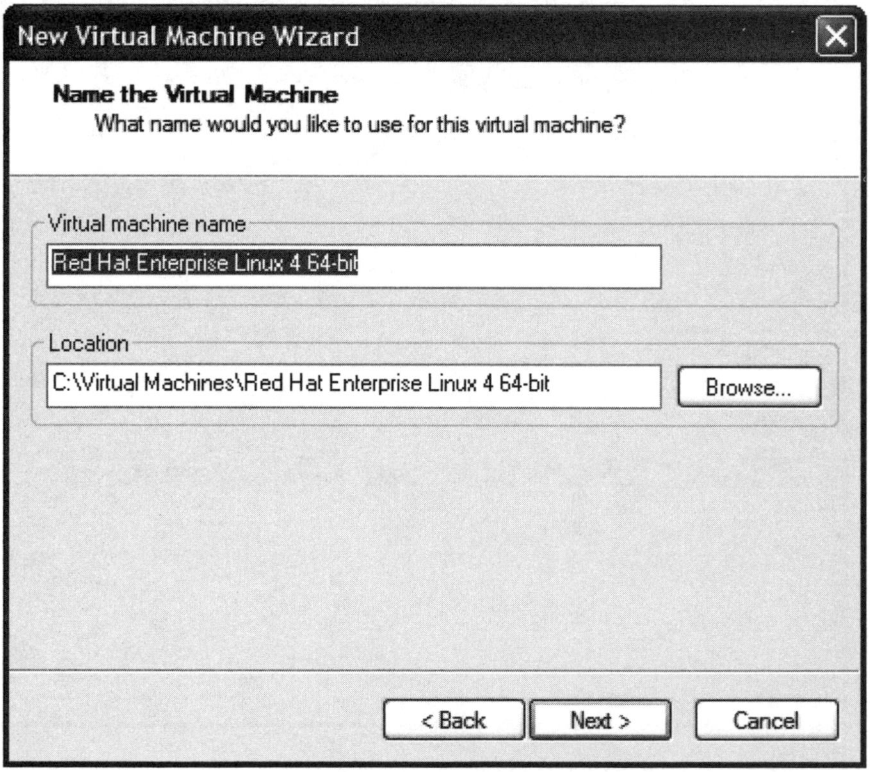

Figure 4.2: *Naming the Virtual Machine*

The only consideration here is to name the VM something that is both appropriate and memorable and to place this information in a place that is easy to backup or zip. The default is to place this information in "My Documents\My Virtual Machines." But like many default settings, it is not advisable to use this value. It is much better to define a standard for your organization, such as:

- Windows D:\Virtual Machines
- Linux/Unix /VirtualMachines

This means that anybody working on the VM infrastructure will know exactly where to find VM images regardless of the host operating system. In all the above cases, it is also advisable to place these VM images on a second, non-system and non-swap disk drive. Placement of the actual database content files will be covered later in this chapter.

The third step covers networking. While VMware offers many options, it is advisable to again stick with one enterprise-wide standard that is easy to implement, generally accessible, readily remembered, and straightforwardly portable. The best choice here is NAT: Network Address Translation, as shown in Figure 4.3.

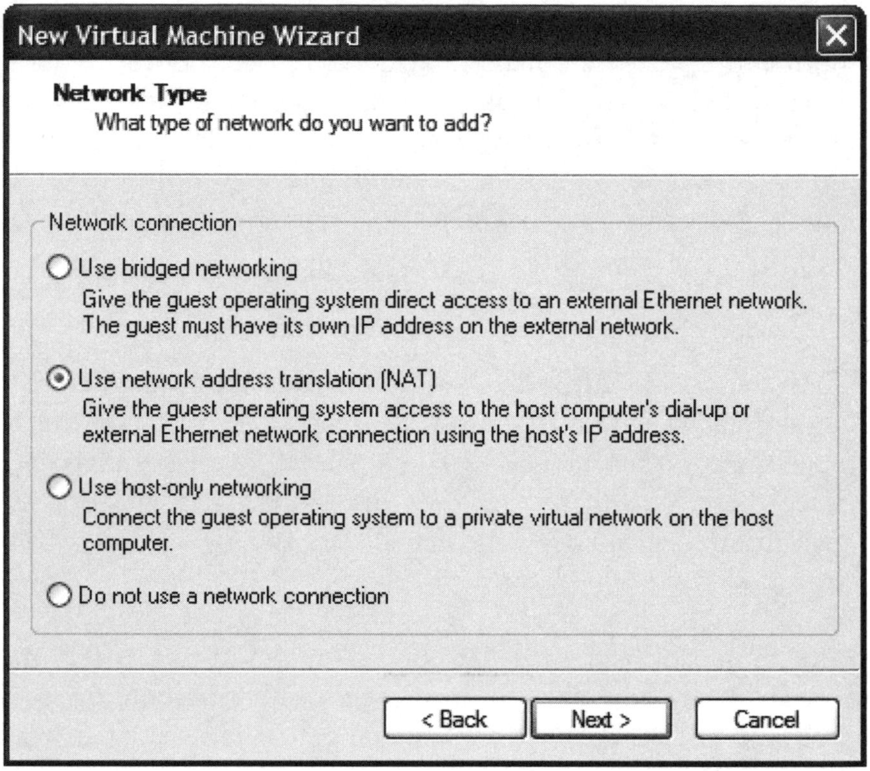

New Virtual Machine Wizard

Network Type
What type of network do you want to add?

Network connection

- ○ Use bridged networking
  Give the guest operating system direct access to an external Ethernet network. The guest must have its own IP address on the external network.
- ◉ Use network address translation (NAT)
  Give the guest operating system access to the host computer's dial-up or external Ethernet network connection using the host's IP address.
- ○ Use host-only networking
  Connect the guest operating system to a private virtual network on the host computer.
- ○ Do not use a network connection

< Back | Next > | Cancel

Figure 4.3: *Network Type*

Think of NAT as simply DHCP (Dynamic Host Configuration Protocol) between the host server and its guest operating systems. That means it is both generally accessible and readily portable. Plus, it is really nothing more than an extension of an existing network technology standard (i.e. DHCP) already in use by many organizations. Using a network technology based upon abstraction achieves a very logical and natural fit to the virtualized environment.

A logical question is "why none of the other choices?" The fourth choice, no network, obviously makes little sense since an Oracle database needs to be accessible to the outside world. The first choice, bridged network, requires each guest to have its own

IP address and many organizations have tried to move away from this network infrastructure model for both security and manageability reasons. The third choice, host-only network, could be used but only under the circumstance where the host server implements DHCP to route/redirect public network traffic to its own private network. But now there is an assumption that a host operating system that readily provides such capability exists – and further assuming no hypervisor. Both assumptions fly contrary to the keep it generic and portable ideals.

The fourth step is to create the disk space necessary to hold the guest operating system base install (and just that space), as shown in Figure 4.4.

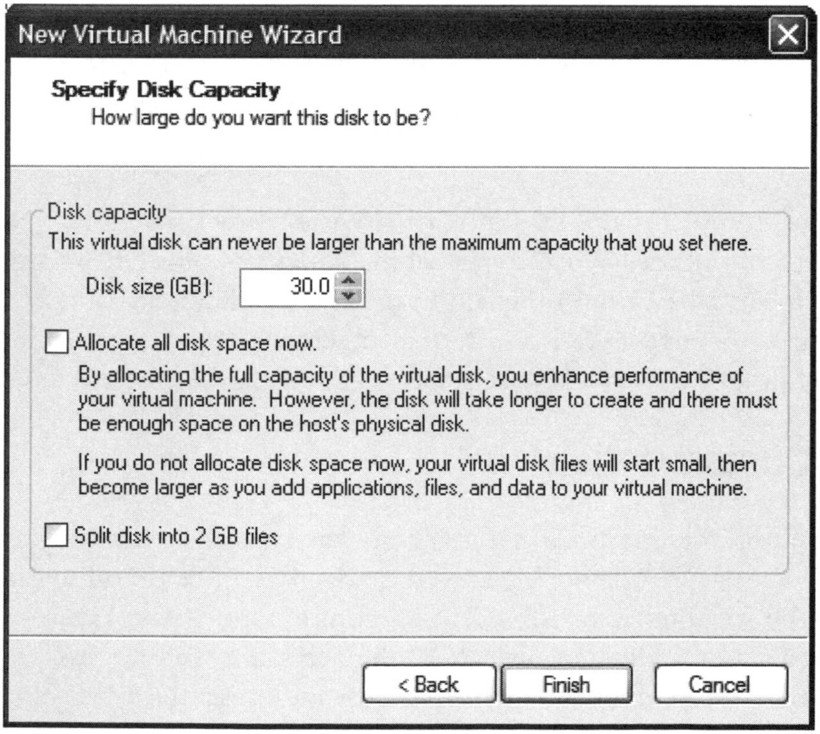

Figure 4.4: *Creating Disk Capacity*

Disk capacity should be selected to hold the guest operating system install, swap space, OS patches or updates, temporary work space, and Oracle install. With disk space being so cheap these days, err on the side of too big. Most operating systems and Oracle can fit nicely in 30-40 GBs of disk space and the cost for this allocation amount is acceptable, even if it does err on the side of being, relatively speaking, excessively wasteful.

During this fourth step, the first obvious and critical performance alternative is encountered: preallocate or virtually allocate the disk space? Since it is not recommended to place the operating system files and actual database content (i.e. table and index file) on the same virtual disk, this question is somewhat simpler. The minimal performance gain for pre-allocating the operating system disk is generally offset by the improved portability of not requiring a specified minimum size. But with cheap disk space and such a relatively small size here, it is the DBA's call. There is just not enough blood in the turnip to overly concentrate on optimizing this aspect further.

That completes the creations of a basic virtual machine. Note that not only are VMware virtual machines portable across any of their virtualization products, but numerous competitors offer the ability to import VMware virtual machines into their products' technology due to VMware's commanding market share.

VM Customization

Creating the empty virtual machine was the quick and easy part. Now as a DBA deploying an Oracle database in a virtual world, it is the customization of the VM configuration parameters that need to be addressed next. Like the section before, limits posed at the VM settings level often cannot be overcome by operating system or database tuning efforts. Once again, it is extremely important to get these settings right the very first time, so do not skip or make light of this step either!

There are a lot of configuration settings to cover – so it is time to get started!

The first virtual machine setting that must be defined is how much memory to allocate to the virtual machine. In this case, the minimum (32MB), recommended (384MB), and maximum permissible (3580MB) memory allocations are shown in Figure 4.5. The maximum is based upon the host server's memory setting covered in the prior chapter. In this example, Red Hat Linux guest OS will be selected to support running two Oracle instances, their background processes, and the requisite number of dedicated server process for development and test databases. Two gigabytes has been set aside for the virtual machine.

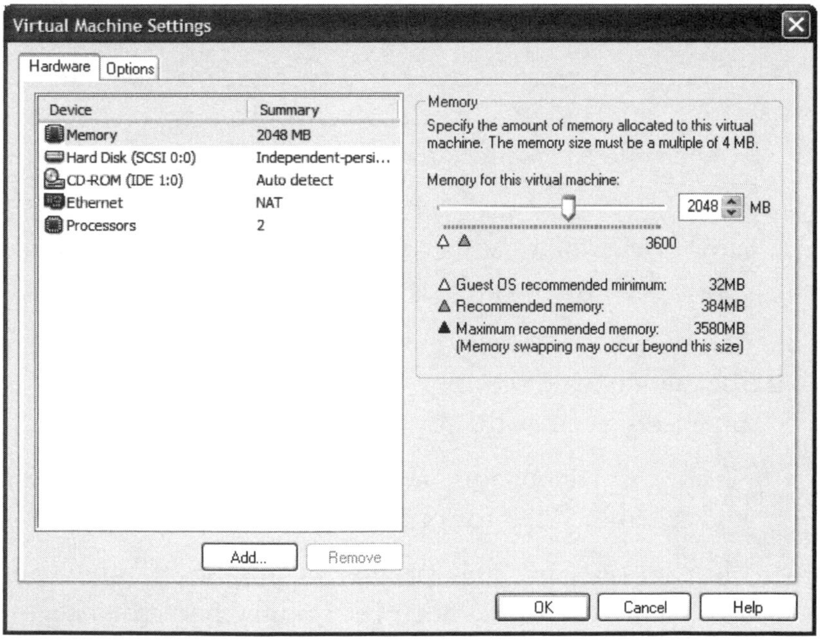

Figure 4.5: *Virtual Machine Settings*

Some other key performance related settings to note and adjust for the specific hardware environment and business database needs are:

- "Hardware" tab
    - "Hard Disk" type=SCSI (more portable than IDE)
    - "Hard Disk" mode=independent & persistent (no overhead for snapshot & disk I/Os occurring immediately)
    - Defragment the virtual disk via the VMware defragment utility once the OS and Oracle are installed
    - CD-ROM "Connect at power on"=unchecked (default =checked can slow down both VMware host & guest)
    - "Number of processors" – remember this during guest OS install in case options exist (e.g. Linux SMP kernel)
- "Options" tab
    - If only one guest active at any time on host, then set "Enter full screen mode after powering on"=checked (requires less resources to manage just one active GUI)
    - "Disable Snapshots"=checked (default=unchecked can slow down VM, it's like running database with archive log mode enabled – i.e. more I/O on the virtual server)
    - "Disable memory page trimming"=checked (default=unchecked may impact I/O intensive workloads on guests, such as that by Oracle databases)
    - "Run with debugging information"=unchecked (default and recommended for optimal performance)
    - "Log virtual machine progress periodically"=unchecked (default and recommended for optimal performance)

That is not quite all yet. So far the base virtual machine has been created and customized for some very universal database usage scenarios. But now it is time to add disk space to actually contain the databases' data. In other words, disk drives are needed to provide tablespace allocation regardless of whether file systems, clustered file systems, virtual file systems, raw devices, or Oracle ASM are being used.

The hardware tab's "Add..." button can be utilized to create those additional virtual disks, resulting in the key screen snapshot shown below in Figure 4.6, as well as a few others much like the disk setting screens that have already been shown while creating the virtual machine's first disk drive.

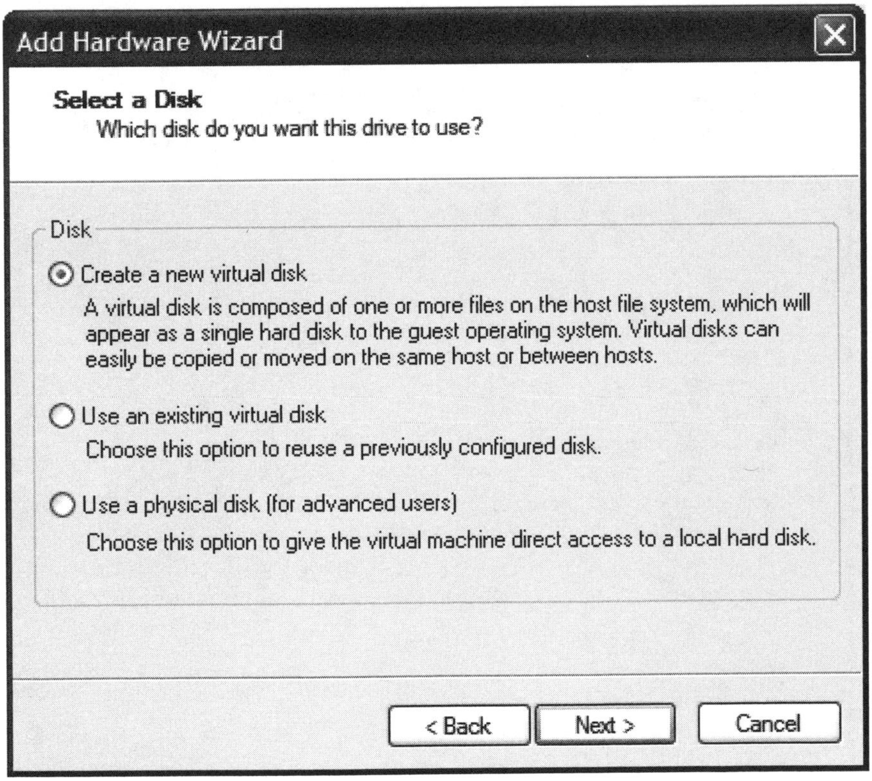

Figure 4.6: *Creating a New Virtual Disk*

To create a *Hard Disk*, choose its nature (physical vs. virtual), its type (IDE vs. SCSI), its size and allocation strategy (pre-allocate vs. dynamic growth). The only new part is the second question, which is what the nature of disk drive is. While an old tried and true DBA paradigm has been to prefer physical or raw devices for optimal performance, that choice would fly contrary to the keep it "generic" and portable ideals. So only if it is performance at all costs, no matter what, choose physical disk, which permits the allocation of an entire disk or partition to a virtual disk.

However, one virtual disk creation task is performed differently when allocating disk space for Oracle data files. Namely, choose to pre-allocate those virtual disks as shown below in Figure 7.

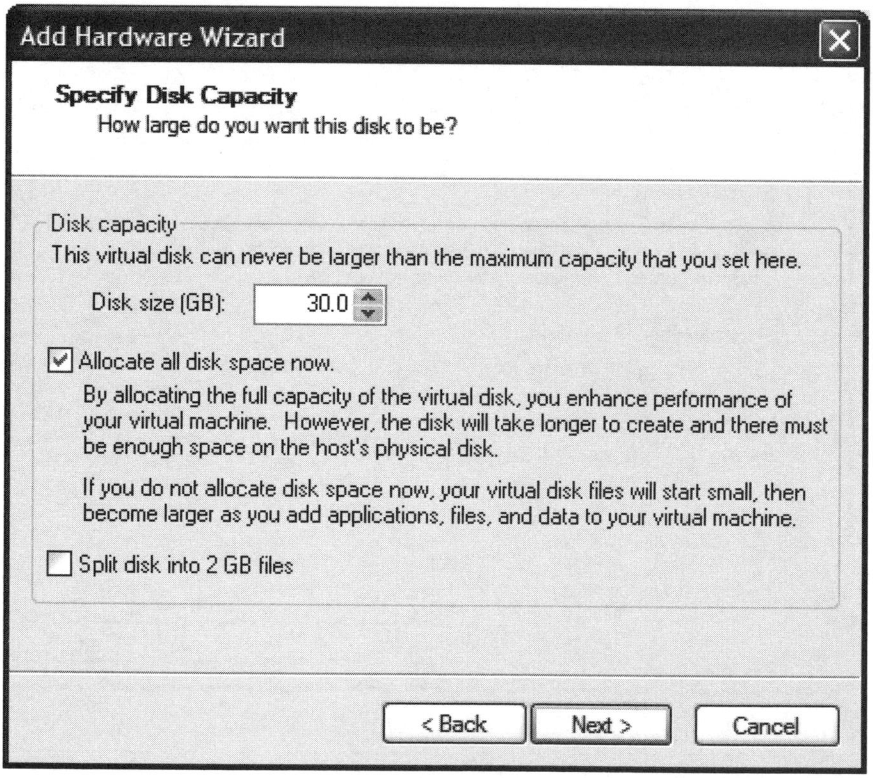

Add Hardware Wizard

Specify Disk Capacity
How large do you want this disk to be?

Disk capacity
This virtual disk can never be larger than the maximum capacity that you set here.
Disk size (GB): 30.0

[x] Allocate all disk space now.
By allocating the full capacity of the virtual disk, you enhance performance of your virtual machine. However, the disk will take longer to create and there must be enough space on the host's physical disk.

If you do not allocate disk space now, your virtual disk files will start small, then become larger as you add applications, files, and data to your virtual machine.

[ ] Split disk into 2 GB files

< Back | Next > | Cancel

Figure 4.7: *Allocating Disk Space*

The reason is quite simple – Oracle pre-allocates or formats disk space allocated to tablespaces with all the requisite blocks to populate the data file for its given size. So if 30 GB is going to be allocated to the tablespace's data file, then it makes sense to pre-allocate it at the virtual level since Oracle is just going to format all that space immediately anyhow. And if the DBA was considering stopping short, perhaps by creating the data file at only 20GB, why pay twice for the data file to extend dynamically at both the virtual and Oracle levels? Once is sufficient!

Incremental Guest Tuning

Now a properly configured and optimized virtual machine exists for Oracle database server usage. The next step is to tune the guest operating system both for virtualization and Oracle database usage. It is really no different than tuning a stand-alone database server. It is important to account for correctly setting configuration files, operating system parameters, and database parameters as always. The only difference is that CPU, memory, and I/O assumptions need to be made a little more "generically" since the hardware has been abstracted and may probably change over time. So the preference is to have all tuning efforts apply relatively well going forward, when available computing resources may increase.

The only ancillary complexity is that there may be multiple databases using some shared resources, much like historically hosting multiple databases on a single box, and they need to be accounted for that at some point during tuning. But each optimization step should occur in its own due time. Tune the virtual server first, and then tune each of the virtual machines as though single database per server deployments are being done. Technically speaking, this could occur at some point even in a virtual world. And finally, tune the guest operating system and

Oracle database for side effects caused by sharing resources, but do not start here or try to do it all in one pass.

As with any scientific experiment or database benchmarking, only a single variable per test iteration should be changed so that the results can be properly measured and observed. This technique is called Incremental Tuning and it is suggested that this is both the mandatory and only reliable way to correctly optimize any computer system, especially a virtualized one being used for a database.

Optimize by Subsystem

It is best to think of a database server as being composed of four basic subsystems, which should be the focus of any operating system tuning efforts:

- CPU
- Memory
- I/O
- Network

Furthermore, all the above areas should be tuned with the server's purpose in mind – hosting an Oracle database. The basic idea is that the overall performance can be no better or worse than the sum of its parts. Plus, all of the above are possibly dynamic in the virtual world, so again making more generic assumptions should generally lead to better aggregate results. This is really nothing more than Incremental Tuning applied at the first granular level of interest: the subsystems.

The process for doing just this for both Linux and Windows will be explored next. All these techniques would apply in some fashion to other operating systems such as Sun Solaris, Hewlett Packard's HP-UX or IBM's AIX. In all cases, it is assumed that

Oracle pre- and post-install steps are being fully and correctly done. So the following are in addition to Oracle's default recommendations. A summarization is included at the end of the chapter as well for future quick reference.

Optimizing Linux

Tuning Linux for proper CPU setup is actually quite easy – there are just two items to address. First, make sure to install the correct address space version to match the CPU architecture (i.e. 32-bit vs. 64-bit). While this may not make a substantial and directly measurable impact, it is simply that 64-bit environments offer larger address spaces and thus larger SGAs, which can often potentially reduce overall I/O. Second, make sure to always install the SMP kernel regardless of the hardware. A single CPU running an SMP kernel will suffer a very small but acceptable performance penalty. But remember the goal here is to think more generically as tuning is being done. Today's single may well be tomorrow's double or even quad. To best reap those potential performance rewards, one should err on the side of potentially more CPUs in the future.

Optimizing Linux memory usage is much like the CPU - assume the minimum requirements to meet the business SLA needs, but keep in mind that it could grow at any time. However, unlike the CPU where one can simply choose the single option for SMP kernel to cover all bases, there are potentially two choices with regard to memory configuration.

If using 32-bit Linux, then the address space is limited by hardware to 4GB with a Linux imposed split of 3GB for user space and 1GB for kernel space. However, there are some well known "workarounds" as shown in the following table. These are also well documented on Oracle's metalink web site and in numerous Oracle book & papers. But the days of 32-bit are numbered, so it is better to accept the inevitable and adopt 64-bit as soon as possible.

KERNEL TYPE	TOTAL RAM	SGA LIMIT	WORK AROUND
Uniprocessor or SMP	<4GB	1.70GB	None – Default
Uniprocessor or SMP	<4GB	2.00GB	Low SGA Attach Address
Uniprocessor or SMP	<4GB	2.70GB	In-Memory File System
SMP– normalmem	16GB	14.00GB	In-Memory File System
SMP– hugemem	<4GB	2.70GB	None – Default
SMP– hugemem	<4GB	3.42GB	Low SGA Attach Address
SMP– hugemem	>4GB	3.42GB	Low SGA Attach Address
SMP– hugemem	64GB	62.00GB	In-Memory File System

Table 4.1: *Examples of Workarounds*

Of course, if 64-bit Linux is being used, this entire memory issue is essentially eliminated. However, there is one more little tweak that can be applied to either 32-bit or 64-bit Oracle servers and that is the use of Huge Pages. This Linux 2.6 kernel feature simply utilizes larger than the 4K pages to reduce virtual memory I/O operations when working with lots of memory. Here are some documented limits:

HARDWARE PLATFORM	KERNEL 2.4	KERNEL 2.6
Linux x86 (IA32)	4MB	4MB
Linux x86-64 (AMD64, EM64T)	2MB	2MB
Linux Itanium (IA64)	256MB	256MB
IBM Power Based Linux (PPC64)	NA	16MB
IBM zSeries Based Linux	NA	NA
IBM S/390 Based Linux	NA	NA

Table 4.2: *Documented limits of Hugh Pages*

The process to enable Huge Pages is as follows:

- X = grep Hugepagesize /proc/meminfo
- Y = Largest (MB of all client SGA's) * 1024
- Z = # Huge Pages needed = Y / X
- Set Huge Page Pool size
  - edit /etc/sysctl.conf
  - vm.nr_hugepages = Z
- Increase ulimit parameter "*memlock*" for oracle user
  - edit /etc/security/limits.conf
  - oracle soft memlock Y
  - oracle hard memlock Y
- reboot

Interestingly enough, many people with killer 64-bit servers increase their SGA size without implementing Huge Pages. The results have been well documented in Oracle's metalink document id = 361670.1 where SGA sizes greater than 10GB have displayed decreases in performance! So as a general practice, always implement Huge Pages.

To improve I/O for file system based Oracle data files, Linux offers a little known and seldom used option that can yield between 50-150% performance improvements in standard database benchmarks like the TPC-C. Try simply changing the /etc/fstab file entries for the Oracle data file mount points as follows:

- For ext2 and 3 file systems, add "*,noatime*" to the third column

What this does is tell the operating system that it is not necessary to update the *last access time* for directories and files under that mount point, which translates into radically reduced total I/O.

Since the Oracle background processes are already accessing the data files every three seconds and have their own headers with timestamps within them, why spend I/O resources to update time attributes for files or directories?

To improve I/O for ASM based oracle data files, simply double the default SGA sizing parameter for the ASM instance from 64MB to 128MB. Memory is far too cheap these days to haggle over such a small amount. And the obvious results will more than justify the cost.

Optimizing Windows

As with Linux, Microsoft Windows offers some very simple yet highly productive tweaks that can be universally applied to any Windows virtual machine's guest operating system install. And interestingly, some are conceptually the same as in the prior Linux section with just a different setting or syntax to accomplish the same tweak.

Tuning Windows for proper CPU setup is actually quite easy – there are just two items to address. First, make sure to install the correct address space version to match the CPU architecture (i.e. 32-bit vs. 64-bit). This has not been found to make a substantial and directly measurable impact. It is simply that 64-bit environments offer larger address spaces and thus larger SGAs, which can often potentially reduce overall I/O. Second and most importantly, if possible standardize on Microsoft Windows 2003 Enterprise Edition Release 2 and make sure to install the specific version of Oracle for that platform. Because as much as it pains a Linux bigot to admit, Windows 2003 Enterprise with the right version of Oracle installed gives Linux a run for its money. There will not be any earth shattering results published here so as not to get in any trouble or start any religious wars, but on the next page is a chart that has been used in some database benchmarking papers when comparing the various operating systems.

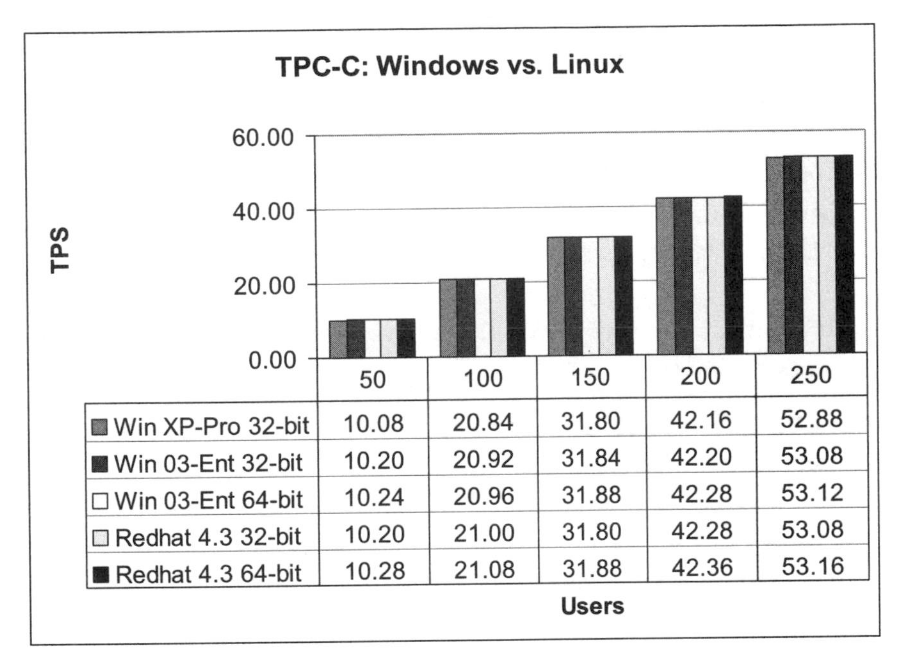

	50	100	150	200	250
Win XP-Pro 32-bit	10.08	20.84	31.80	42.16	52.88
Win 03-Ent 32-bit	10.20	20.92	31.84	42.20	53.08
Win 03-Ent 64-bit	10.24	20.96	31.88	42.28	53.12
Redhat 4.3 32-bit	10.20	21.00	31.80	42.28	53.08
Redhat 4.3 64-bit	10.28	21.08	31.88	42.36	53.16

Figure 4.8: *Comparing Windows vs. Linux*

The conclusion is clear: choose the database platform based upon the current hardware and staffing assets. If the systems people currently know and are comfortable with Windows, then why suffer learning and embracing a new OS when the performance is essentially the same? However, note that the above results were accomplished using the standard Oracle Windows binaries and not the Windows 2003 specific versions. It is clear that Oracle on Windows 2003 is a completely viable platform.

To improve I/O for file system based Oracle data files, Windows offers a little known and seldom used option that can yield between 50-150% performance improvements in standard database benchmarks like the TPC-C by simply changing the Windows registry setting as follows:

- HKEY_LOCAL_MACHINE\System\CurrentControlSet\Control\FileSystem\ NtfsDisableLastAccessUpdate=1

What this does is set the operating system to *Disable Last Access Update* for directories and files on this Windows server, which translates into radically reduced total I/O. Since the Oracle background processes are accessing the data files every three seconds anyway and have their own headers with timestamps within them, why spend I/O resources to update time attributes for files or directories?

Some other common Windows registry tweaks for database servers include:

- Disable 8 dot 3 Name Creation - This setting controls whether MS-DOS compatible 8.3 file names should be generated on NTFS partitions. Disabling this feature can increase the performance on high usage partitions that have large amount of files with long filenames. Setting this option also toggles whether to permit extended characters to be used in 8.3 filenames.
- Enable a large size file system cache - This entry controls whether the system maintains a standard size or a large size file system cache. Enabling a larger cache makes sense for networked database servers with sufficient memory.
- Disable paging of the kernel code - This entry controls whether the user and kernel mode drivers and the kernel mode core system code itself can be paged. Disabling the paging of kernel code makes sense for database servers with sufficient memory.
- I/O Page Lock Limit - This entry controls the maximum amount of RAM that can be locked for I/O operations. The default minimizes RAM usage. An I/O intensive system could benefit from larger buffer sizes. Caution: setting this

parameter too high can result in slower performance. Set it in increments and see how it affects the system.

The corresponding recommended registry settings are as follows:

- HKEY_LOCAL_MACHINE\System\CurrentControlSet\Control\FileSystem\NtfsDisable8dot3NameCreation = 1
- HKEY_LOCAL_MACHINE\System\CurrentControlSet\Control\FileSystem\NtfsAllowExtendedCharacterIn8dot3Name = 0
- HKEY_LOCAL_MACHINE\System\CurrentControlSet\Control\SessionManager\MemoryManagement\LargeSystemCache = 1
- HKEY_LOCAL_MACHINE\System\CurrentControlSet\Control\SessionManager\MemoryManagement\DisablePagingExecutive=1
- HKEY_LOCAL_MACHINE\System\CurrentControlSet\Control\SessionManager\Memory Management\IoPageLockLimit = N, where N is chosen as follows:
    - if RAM <= 32MB then
    - IoPageLockLimit = 512
    - if RAM > 32MB then
    - IoPageLockLimit = 4K
    - if RAM > 64MB then
    - IoPageLockLimit = 8K
    - if RAM > 128MB then
    - IoPageLockLimit = 16K
    - if RAM > 160MB then
    - IoPageLockLimit = 32K

- if RAM > 256MB then
- IoPageLockLimit = 64K

Note that included on the book's DVD and download website is a free Windows program to easily set all these parameters on both local and remote database server as shown below.

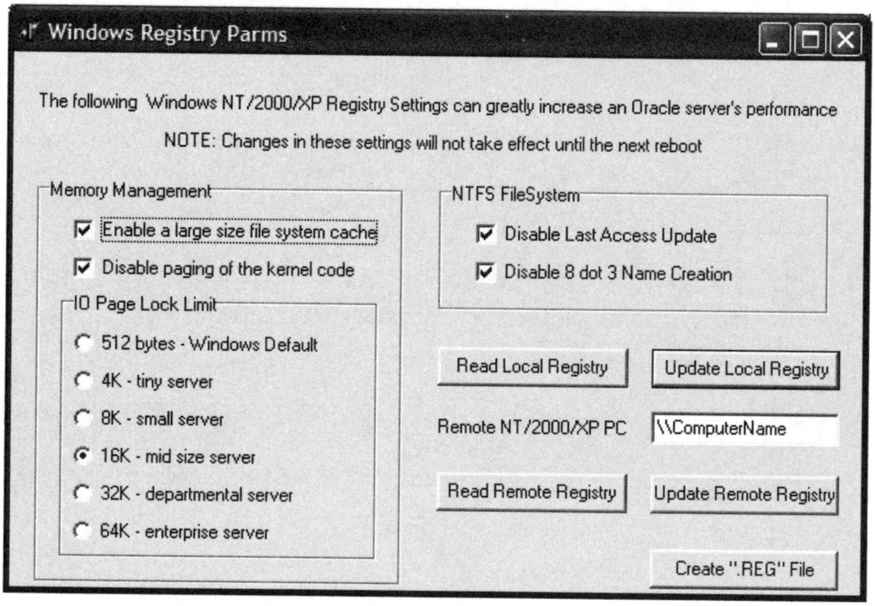

Figure 4.9: *Windows Registry Settings*

To improve I/O for ASM based oracle data files, simply double the default SGA sizing parameter for the ASM instance from 64MB to 128MB. Memory is far too cheap these days to haggle over such a small amount. As stated before, the results will more than justify the cost.

Quick Reference

Below is a summary of the recommended client OS optimizations:

Linux:

- Kernel
  - 64-bit
  - SMP Support
- Memory
  - Huge Pages
  - In-Memory File System
- I/O
  - /etc/fstab add *",noatime"*
  - Double ASM SGA size

Windows:

- Version
  - 64-bit
  - Windows 2003 Enterprise R2
- Oracle
  - 64-bit
  - Windows 20003 specific version
- Registry (use my freeware program to update)
  - Disable last access update
  - Disable 8 dot 3 name creation
  - Enable large size file system cache
  - Disable paging of kernel code
  - IO Page Lock Limit >= 16K

Conclusion

In this chapter, the options to best configure the client virtual machines and their guest operating systems in order to maximize database performance have been explored. All of these techniques should be considered as "Best Practices" and liberally implemented across all virtual machines and their guest operating systems. The cost to implement each of these concepts is relatively small, but both their individual and cumulative performance impacts are well worth the trouble.

Oracle 11g Setup

CHAPTER 5

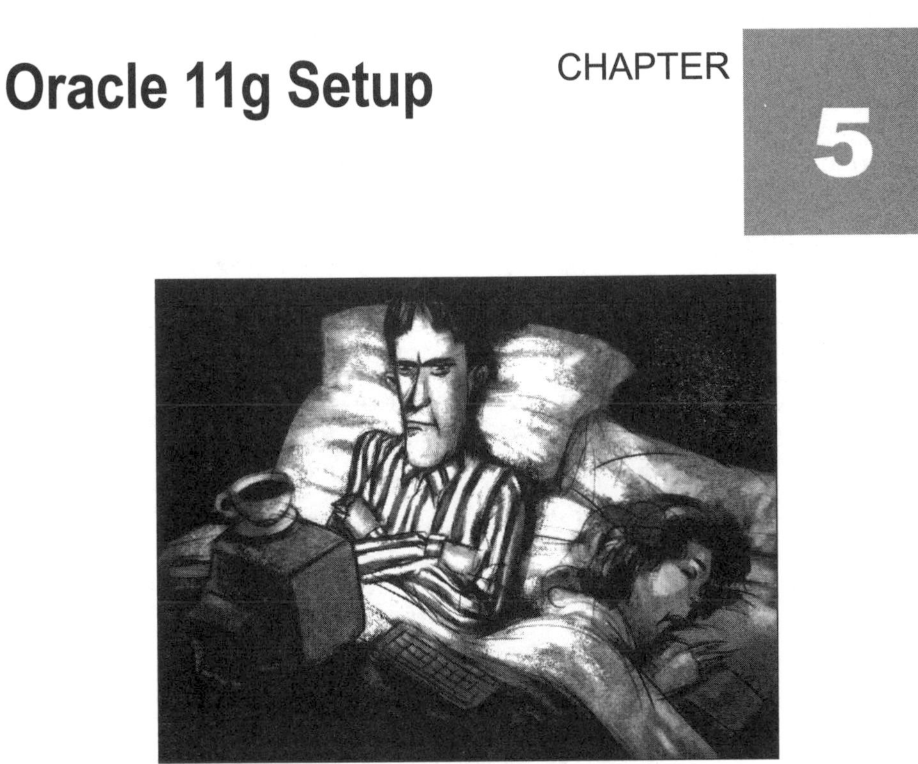

Installing Oracle requires constant vigilance!

Overview

Sometimes a cartoon can ring truer than ever expected – like the one above. Oracle makes the graphical installer pretty foolproof these days. What this means is that the DBA can feel pretty foolish when he runs into issues and then remembers what obvious thing he forgot. Having worked with Oracle for over twenty years, this author still makes these kind of silly mistakes more than a few times. But those days are now gone with VMware images. The DBA can get a perfect installation of Oracle on Linux nailed down and then simply zip up those files for use anytime they are needed. In fact, it is so nice to work this way that the next time the DBA has a Windows notebook that needs to be reinstalled, why not just install Linux with VMware and then create a Windows *golden image*.

In this chapter, a recipe is going to be created for installing a streamlined Oracle 11g setup. The example in this chapter will make a perfect laptop/notebook demo platform as it should run in a minimal demo machine (e.g. decent single-core CPU with >= 1.5 GB memory). However, if this recipe is not followed, Oracle 11g by default can very easily swamp a laptop/notebook. Remember, it is an enterprise level database that happens to also function on lesser hardware. So it is not advisable to just run the Oracle installer and accept a starter database or accept all default choices by just pressing next repeatedly. Selections need to be fine tuned so that the DBA has some assurance that the Oracle 11g VMware image built on such low-end equipment can be used; otherwise, demos may possibly run too slowly to be useful.

Preparation

This example assumes the installation is for demo purposes on a laptop or notebook. It also assumes that the host operating system, Windows, Linux, or whatever, is already up and running. This means that, unlike a new server, the host machine has its operating system already installed. Thus, this chapter's example will primarily focus on the following steps:

- Host Setup (Chapter 4)
  - Optimize BIOS Settings
  - Operating System Tuning
  - Host Default Settings
  - Virtual Network Settings
- Guest Setup (Chapter 5)
  - Virtual Machine Creation

    - Operating System Install
    - Operating System Tuning
- Oracle Setup
    - Oracle Software Installation
    - Oracle Database Creation
    - Post Install Tasks (e.g. auto-start)

The only step we will be missing here is the host operating system install under *Host Setup* tasks.

Host Setup

Chapter 3 introduced the concept that the host machine is the center of the virtual universe and that all tuning attempts made here would benefit all hosted virtual machines. Therefore, a simple change might yield spectacular results since all virtual machines would benefit in a cumulative fashion. With a laptop/notebook, there is an additional "bang for the buck" since the hardware is so minimal. Basically, a single disk machine with limited memory will benefit most notably from such efforts and, for demos, this can often make or break the engagement.

The first step will be optimizing the BIOS. The following image is a screen snapshot from the main menu of the very common Phoenix-Award BIOS.

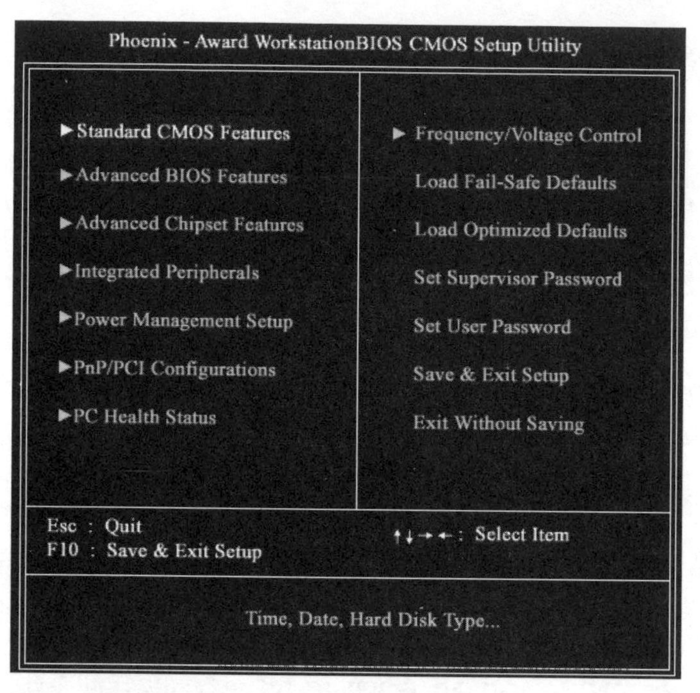

Figure 5.1: *Phoenix-Award BIOS screen*

The two sections that should be visited, the ones that contain settings which provide best bang for the buck, are the Advanced BIOS Features and Advanced Chipset Features. The following options can typically be set:

- Virtualization Technology
- Virus warning
- CPU level 1 cache
- CPU level 2 cache
- APIC mode
- Hyper-Threading
- HDD S.M.A.R.T. capability
- System BIOS cacheable

- Video BIOS cacheable
- Video BIOS shadowing
- Video RAM cacheable

Of course, no two BIOS' menus and screens are the same, but just look for similar items. The good news is that even though the host operating system may already be installed, these changes will take effect on the next reboot without requiring any OS changes. So it is quite safe and easy to make such BIOS optimizations.

Optimizing the host operating system is next. While the system's current performance may be satisfactory, adding VMware, a second operating system, and an Oracle 11g database could well change things. Changing the recommended Windows registry settings using the freeware program on the DVD to modify the default settings to those shown in Figure 5.2 can often yield significant positive results. Plus, like the BIOS settings, these recommendations should not interfere with or negatively impact anything else on the system. Also like those BIOS settings, these changes will not take effect until the next reboot. The only potentially negative side effect could be disabling 8 dot 3 name creation since some older Windows programs could rely upon this. But this is typically not a problem anymore, so making this adjustment should be fine.

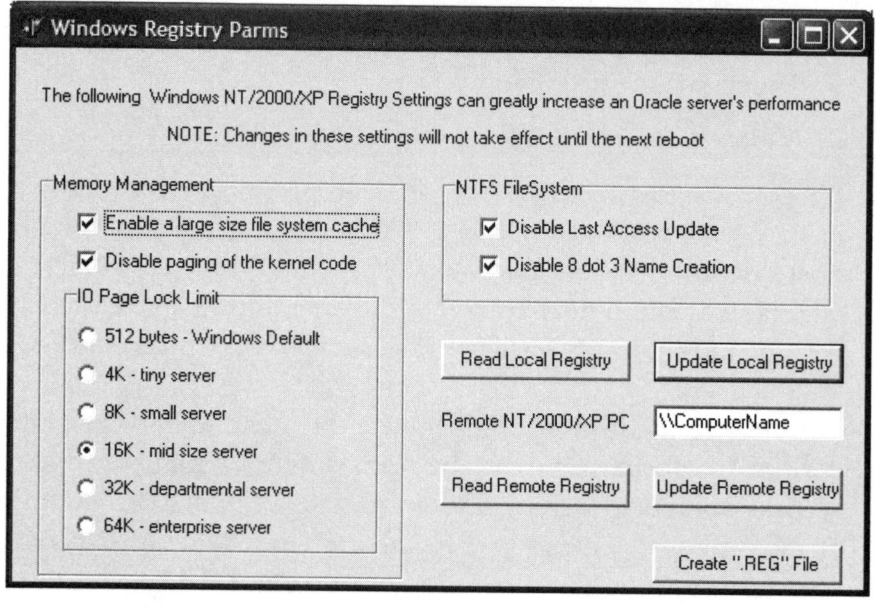

Figure 5.2: *Windows Registry Settings*

It was advised back in Chapter 3 to not install anti-virus and anti-spyware programs on a *minimal server* that might be constructed to serve as a host operating system and hypervisor. Well, in this scenario the system will almost undoubtedly have both already installed and possibly several anti-spyware programs as well. A very critical step here is to exclude the VMware default location for virtual machines from both manual and automatic scans. The default setting in this example is "C:\Virtual Images" so it needs to be excluded in Norton anti-virus as shown in Figure 5.3. And remember, it is best to do so for both automatic, nonstop monitoring and for default manual scans.

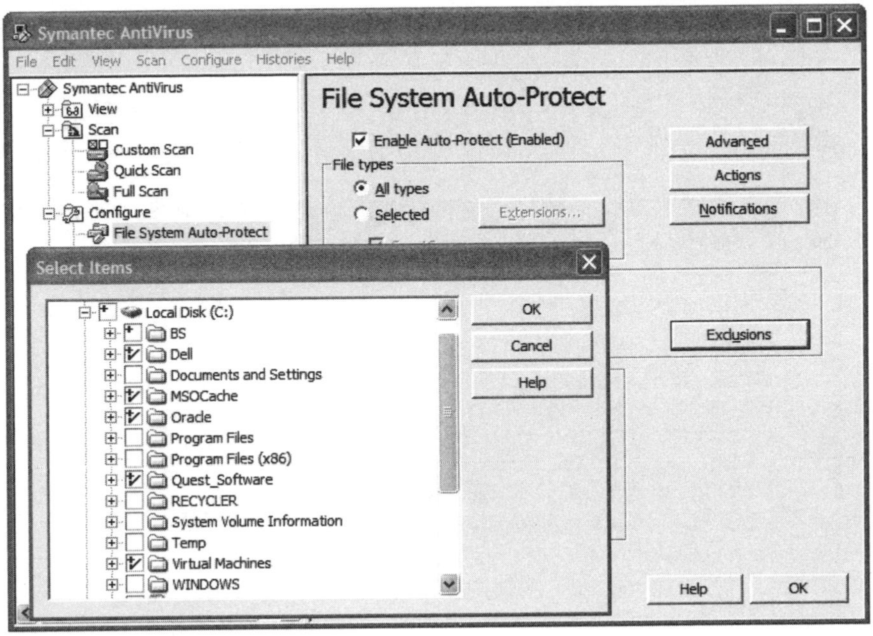

Figure 5.3: *Anti-virus Settings*

Similar exclusions will need to be made in any and all anti-spyware programs such as Webroot Spy Sweeper, PC Tools Spyware Doctor, AVG Anti-Spyware, Spyware Terminator, Spyware Blaster and a host of other similar programs. Unlike anti-virus programs where there is typically just one running, people often run more than one anti-spyware program. Therefore, make sure to properly exclude the VMware default location for virtual machines from both manual and automatic scans for all anti-spyware software.

One last host operating system adjustment that can make a difference, especially on notebooks/laptops, is to exclude the VMware network adapters from Window's firewall protection. Figure 5.4 illustrates this using the standard Windows Firewall software. Make similar adjustment is different firewall programs such as those from Zone Alarm, Kerio or Sygate are being used. The performance gain here will be minimal, but these firewall settings can sometimes interfere with VMware client to host communications. For example, communication between database applications and the Oracle listener. So it is worth the time and effort to set this.

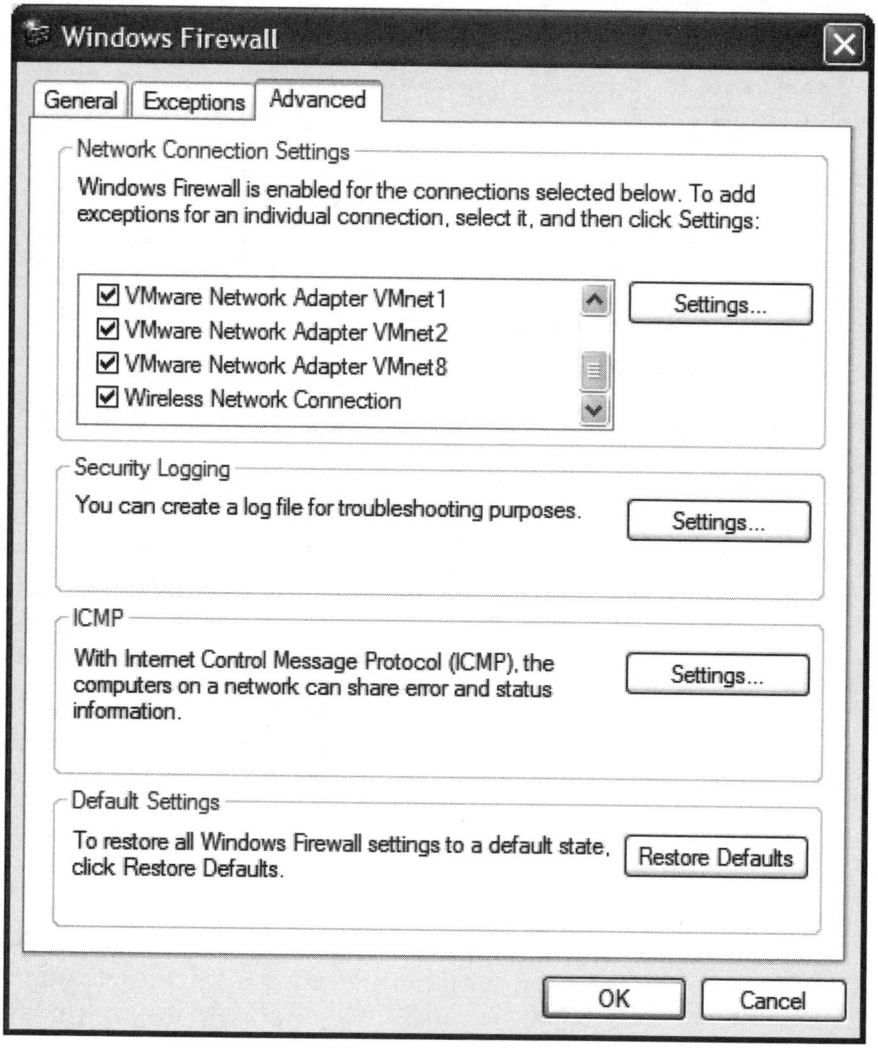

Windows Firewall

General | Exceptions | Advanced

Network Connection Settings

Windows Firewall is enabled for the connections selected below. To add exceptions for an individual connection, select it, and then click Settings:

- VMware Network Adapter VMnet1
- VMware Network Adapter VMnet2
- VMware Network Adapter VMnet8
- Wireless Network Connection

Settings...

Security Logging

You can create a log file for troubleshooting purposes.

Settings...

ICMP

With Internet Control Message Protocol (ICMP), the computers on a network can share error and status information.

Settings...

Default Settings

To restore all Windows Firewall settings to a default state, click Restore Defaults.

Restore Defaults

OK | Cancel

Figure 5.4: *Windows Firewall Preferred Settings*

The final step is to verify the Windows Services settings, i.e. which services start automatically vs. disabled vs. manual, as shown in Figure 4.5. It is best to be very careful here as some of these settings can cause instability or negative side effects. Make sure to only turn off those services that absolutely will not be needed for something else on that laptop/notebook.

Services

File Action View Help

Services (Local)

Name	Description	Status	Startup ...
VMware Authorization Service	Authorizati...	Started	Automatic
VMware DHCP Service	DHCP servi...	Started	Automatic
VMware NAT Service	Network a...	Started	Automatic
VMware Registration Service	Remote ac...	Started	Automatic
VMware Virtual Mount Manager Extended		Started	Automatic
WebClient	Enables Wi...	Started	Automatic
Windows Audio	Manages a...	Started	Automatic
Windows Firewall/Internet Connection Shari...	Provides n...	Started	Automatic
Windows Image Acquisition (WIA)	Provides im...	Started	Automatic
Windows Management Instrumentation	Provides a ...	Started	Automatic
Windows Time	Maintains d...	Started	Automatic
Wireless Configuration	Enables au...		Automatic
Workstation	Creates an...	Started	Automatic
Alerter	Notifies sel...		Disabled
Error Reporting Service	Collects, st...		Disabled
Human Interface Device Access	Enables ge...		Disabled
Indexing Service	Indexes co...		Disabled
Messenger	Transmits ...		Disabled
Net.Tcp Port Sharing Service	Provides a...		Disabled
Routing and Remote Access	Offers rout...		Disabled
System Restore Service	Performs s...		Disabled
Telnet	Enables a r...		Disabled
.NET Runtime Optimization Service v2.0.507...	Microsoft		Manual
.NET Runtime Optimization Service v2.0.507...	Microsoft		Manual
Application Layer Gateway Service	Provides s...	Started	Manual
Application Management	Processes i...		Manual
ASP.NET State Service	Provides s...		Manual

Extended Standard

Figure 5.5: *Windows Services Settings*

The host system should now be fairly well optimized for running VMware.

VMware Host Settings

The next step is to verify that the VMware host software settings are appropriate for the hardware capabilities and software demonstration needs. For this, two areas need to be visited for the VMware host: settings (general options) and virtual network settings. The basic VMware options are fairly straightforward as shown on the next pages in Figures 5.6 and 5.7.

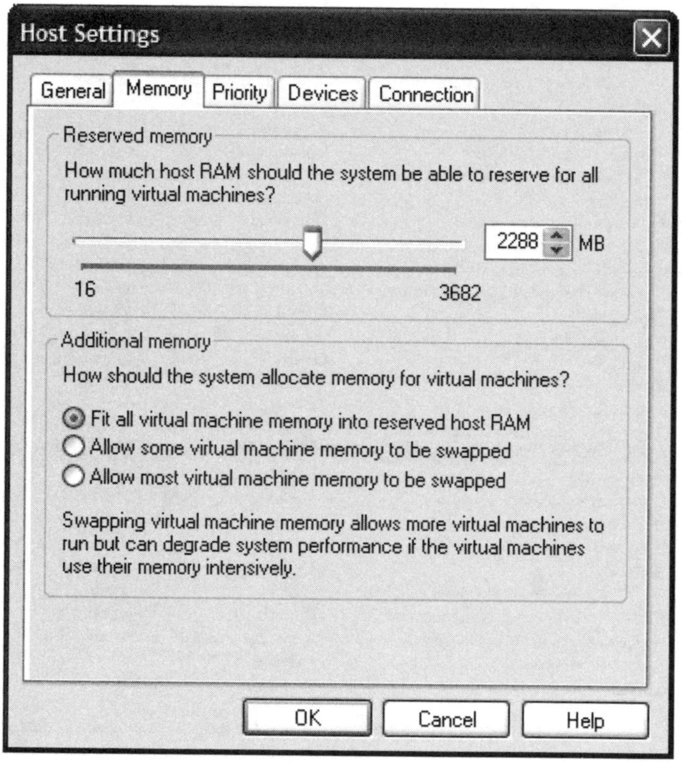

Figure 5.6: *General Host Settings*

Adjustments need to be made on three of the five tabs. Under the "General" tab, set the preferred default location for virtual machines, which you previously made sure to exclude from your anti-virus and anti-spyware monitoring and scans. On the

"Devices" tab, verify that "Disable Auto-Run on the host" is checked. The performance gain here will be minimal, but this setting can often affect virtual machine behavior and stability.

However, it is on the "Memory" tab where the most care needs to be taken in adjusting setting selections. The reserved memory and additional memory settings can have dramatic impact on performance results. Some rules of thumb to follow are: allocate no more than 75% of the total memory, and, if possible, choose to fit the virtual machine into reserved memory without swapping. If the machine has minimal memory or there is a need to run several virtual machines concurrently, this may not be reasonable. It will be necessary to experiment to find the "sweet spot" settings combination.

Now it is time to define the virtual network. While the default settings will work, it is worth taking a few moments to master this section now since it will be critical to when the pseudo and real RAC clusters are created on a single host machine.

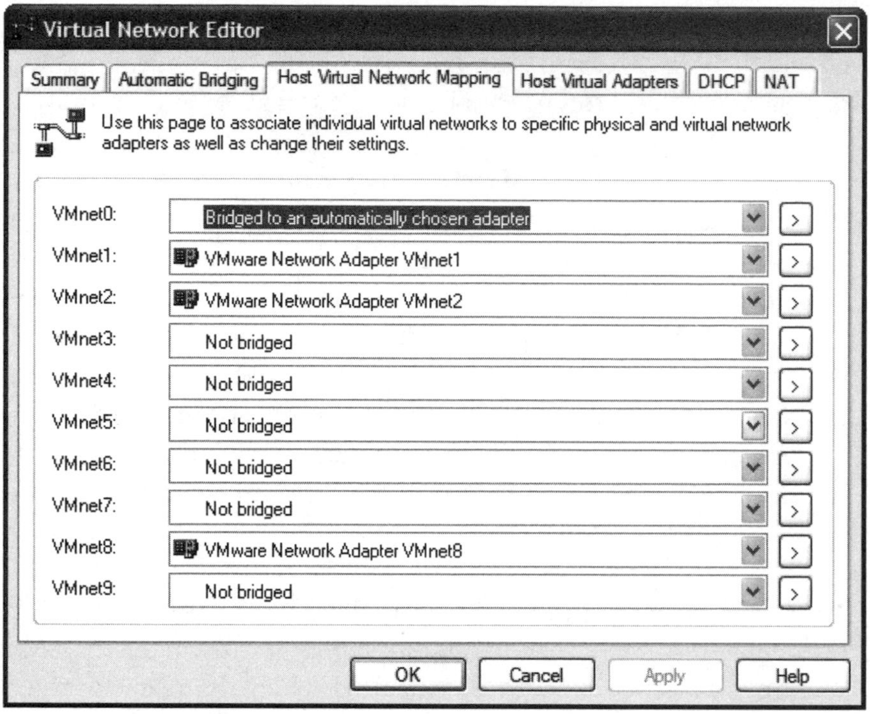

Figure 5.7: *Virtual Network Settings*

In the next section, when the client operating system is installed, start with the virtual machine using the default Network Address Translation (NAT), which is VMnet8, so that the internet can be accessed to apply any patches or updates. After those updates have been applied, you switch to using a user defined network adapter – in this case, VMnet1. There are several reasons for dong this. First, it will be necessary to know network settings for proper RAC configuration. But second, and more importantly, the scenario in this chapter is primarily for doing demos. So internet access will not be needed on the client OS install and updates. Only the host and clients are needed to have the ability to communicate with each other. Therefore, clients can be restricted to a private network, which explains the previous setting to eliminate VMware network adapters from the firewall.

Here are the steps to create a single private network adapter for such purposes. First, visit the Host Virtual Adapters tab and press the "Add" button to create the network adapter. See Figure 5.8. Then press the "Apply" button, which will become enabled after pressing the "OK" button. The reason for doing this is that VMware needs to create the network adapter under Windows as a loopback adapter under VMware control.

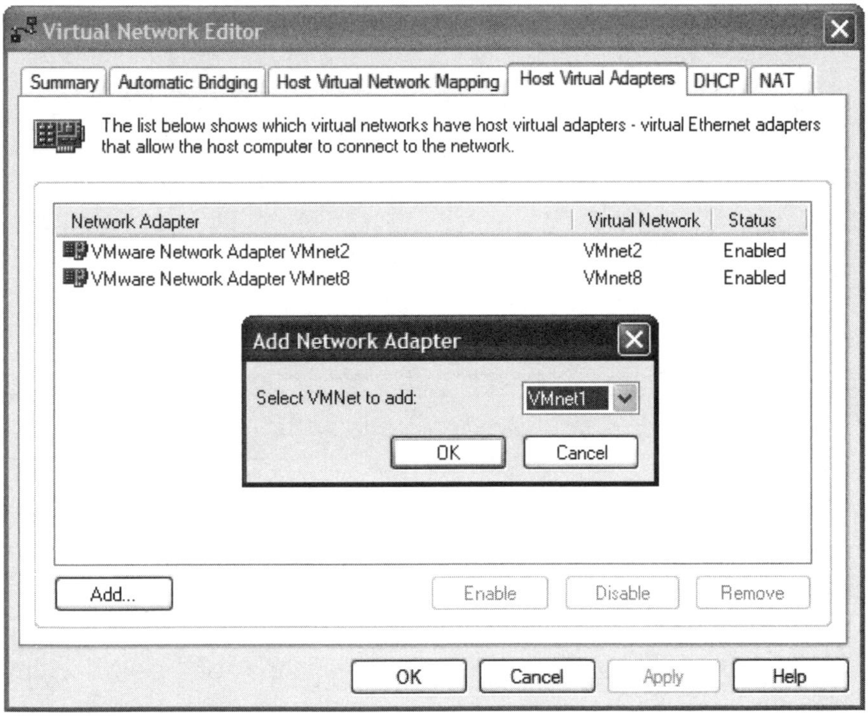

Figure 5.8: *Creating Network Adapter*

Second, visit the "DHCP" tab to define the private network's properties by choosing VMnet1 and pressing the "Properties" button (Figure 5.9). For this example, choose the following network properties settings shown in Figure 5.9.

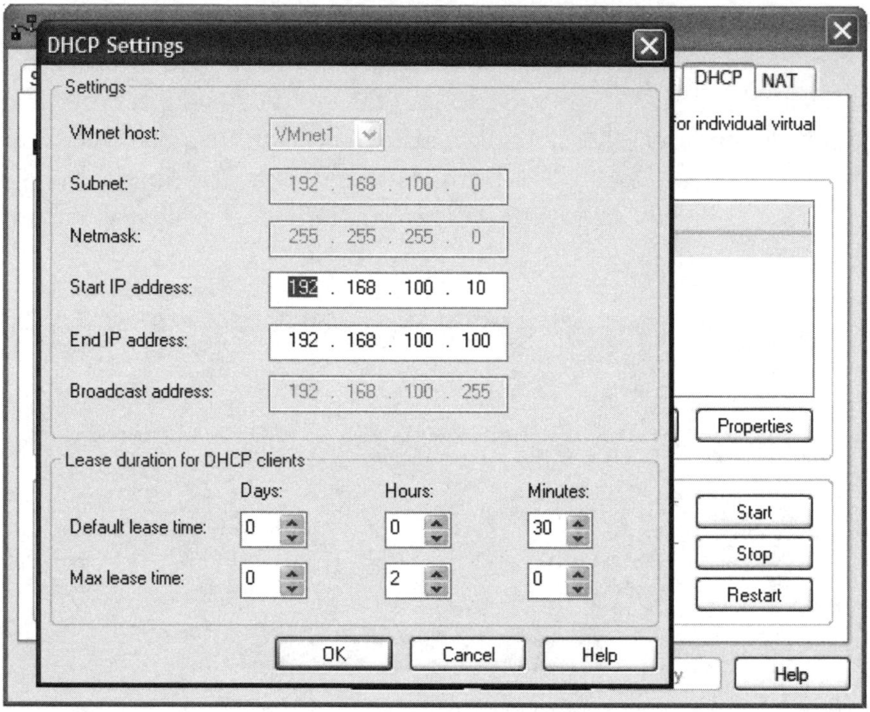

Figure 5.9: *Defining Private Networks Properties*

The private network will be based upon 192.168.100.0 as the subnet. VMware controlled DHCP management will be defined to reserve addresses 192.168.100.10 through 192.168.100.100 for dynamic address allocation. The reason for choosing these values is for hard coding IP addresses for laptop/notebook scenarios. The following IP addresses from the Windows hosts file on the laptop/notebook are used for doing demos:

```
# Laptop/Notebook Demo HOSTS file
#
127.0.0.1                  localhost
192.168.100.101     linux
192.168.100.102     linux_10g
192.168.100.103     linux_11g
192.168.100.104     linux_rac
```

The example in this Chapter involves doing an Oracle 11g setup so the address 192.168.100.103 will be used with an alias of linux_11g. The reason to hard code IP's for demo machines is for fast setup. The VMware directory can be copied to any machine with just three requirements to get it up and running: (1) define the network adapter, (2) add those IP entries to the Windows hosts file, and (3) add the Oracle database SID from the linux_11g virtual machine to the local tnsnames file. After that, everything else will just work. It will be possible then to unzip a backup and get the demo working in a matter of moments.

Virtual Machine Setup

The only exceptions to Chapter 4's recommendations are related to the virtual machine's network settings, such as specifying a private network (i.e. host-only) versus using VMware sponsored DHCP. For this example, the laptop/notebook demo will only involve Windows host application to VMware client Oracle database or another VMware client application to VMware client Oracle database, so internet or public network access are not needed. Only the Ethernet setting modification shown in Figure 5.10 is needed. Simply choose a custom network adapter of VMnet1, which was defined in a prior section. Also note that this setup is defined to run in a very minimal scenario, i.e. a laptop/notebook with just one CPU and 1 GB of client memory.

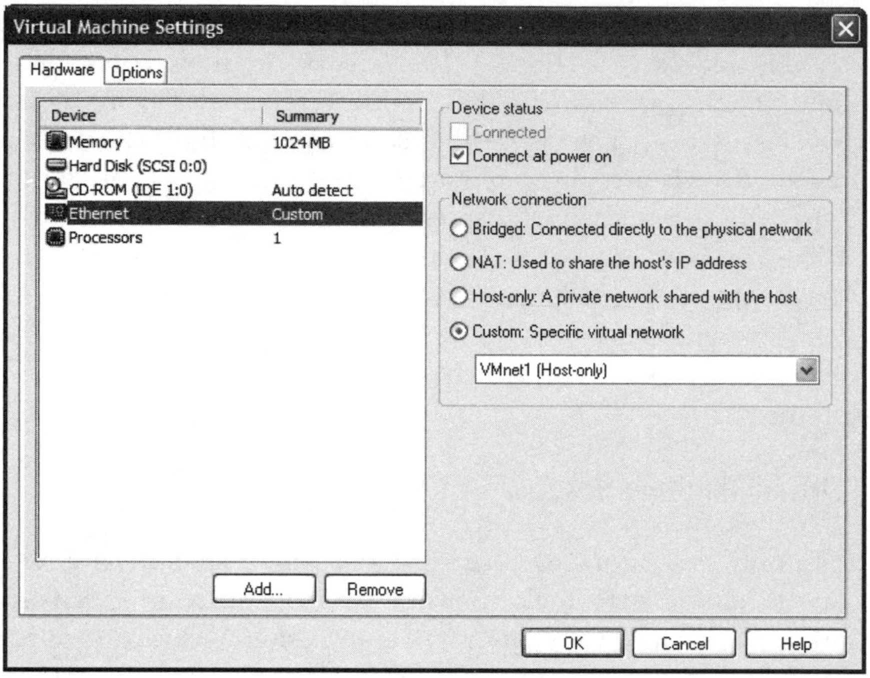

Figure 5.10: *Ethernet Setting Modification*

Client Operating System

For simple demo purposes, Linux makes a very good OS choice. It is free, Oracle is primarily developed there, so new releases and patches come earlier, and it just feels somewhat more realistic to have Windows based applications talking to non-Windows based databases, which is similar to many historically popular Oracle deployment scenarios. While Redhat and SuSE are both popular Oracle Linux platforms, there are some nice free alternatives: CentOS and Oracle's Enterprise Linux. Both are essentially compatible with Redhat and so easy to use with plenty of good reference materials that apply. CentOS is used in this book. This is not a reflection of any superiority of that Linux distribution, it is just that it is close enough to Redhat that is can be used easily for those accustomed to Redhat.

To initiate the OS installation process, simply place the Linux DVD in the laptop's/notebook's DVD drive and tell VMware to start that virtual machine. The process is now essentially 100% the same as if being done on a standalone machine. Some very important Oracle optimizations to make during the Linux installation process and also afterwards will be reviewed.

When asked which type of install to perform, it is generally better to choose a custom Linux install so that only those items that the database setup will need can specifically be picked. Also choose to manually define the partitions. Then, when the "Disk Setup" screen comes up, choose setup values such as those shown in Figure 5.11. The /boot area is where the kernel images are kept to boot the machine. The swap area is kept to a minimum (i.e. 1 GB or swap = RAM), since the objective is to have a very minimal database setup on a limited laptop/notebook for basic demo purposes.

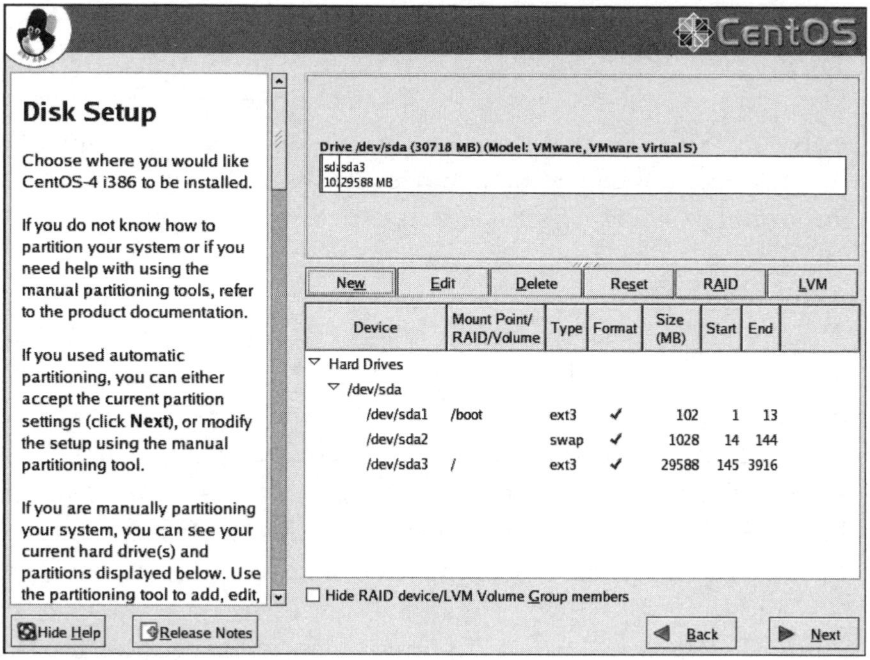

Figure 5.11: *Custom Setup Values*

When the Network Configuration screen appears, define the network as shown in Figure 5.12. Keep in mind that a static IP address for a private network is being chosen, i.e. a VMware host-only connection to the network. Also remember that by using consistent alias names whenever possible throughout the client operating system install process, it will be possible to reproduce this 11g setup quite easily anytime.

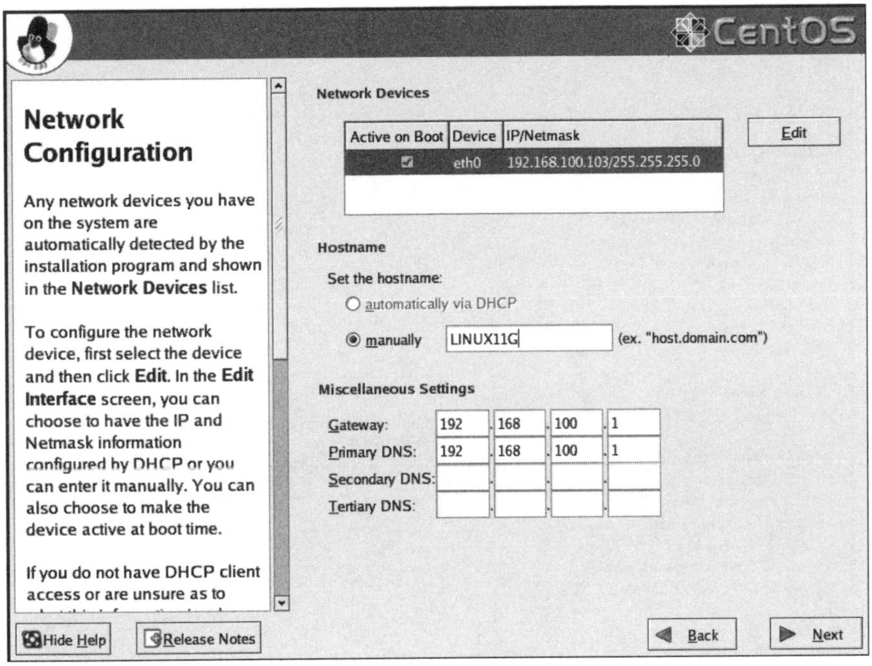

Figure 5.12: *Network Configuration Definitions*

When the Firewall Configuration screen appears, do not enable the client operating system's firewall or Security Enhanced (SE) Linux security options as shown in Figure 5.13. The reason for this is very simple – by creating a private network there will be little or no need for firewall protection. Besides, database server based firewalls just add one additional level of complexity for configuring Oracle because the Oracle listener watches port 1521 by default, which would require opening the port so that database traffic flows unimpeded. Therefore, it is easier to not install the firewall and thus avoid that step. Furthermore, additional overhead on the client operating system will be avoided, which was defined as a critical issue in keeping this system minimal since the objective is to be able to run Oracle 11g on a laptop/notebook for doing demos.

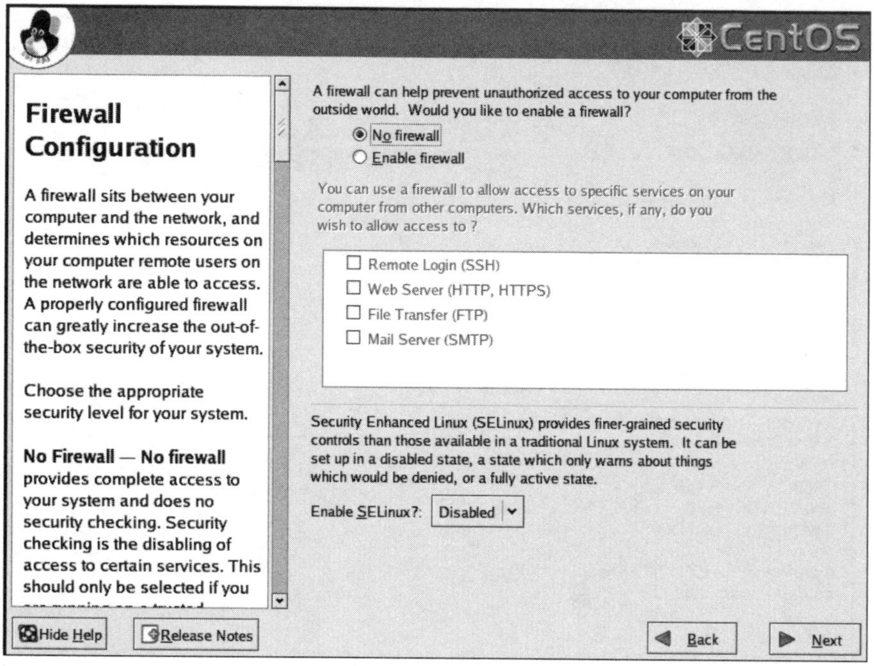

Figure 5.13: *Custom Firewall Configuration*

When the Package Selection screen appears, take the time to choose only those software packages that are absolutely necessary while keeping the selections to a minimum wherever possible. There are two reasons for this. First, the desire is to keep the overhead to a minimum. The more software that is chosen, the more services, demons, or processes that may need to run. And second, the virtual machine is defined using dynamic disk space allocation (i.e. it grows). So the more that is installed, the larger the virtual machine's file on the host will become. While that can slow performance a wee bit, it is the zipping and unzipping delays that quickly become the real issue. The smaller the client, the smaller and faster working with the zip files will be. That can be critical for doing quick rebuilds.

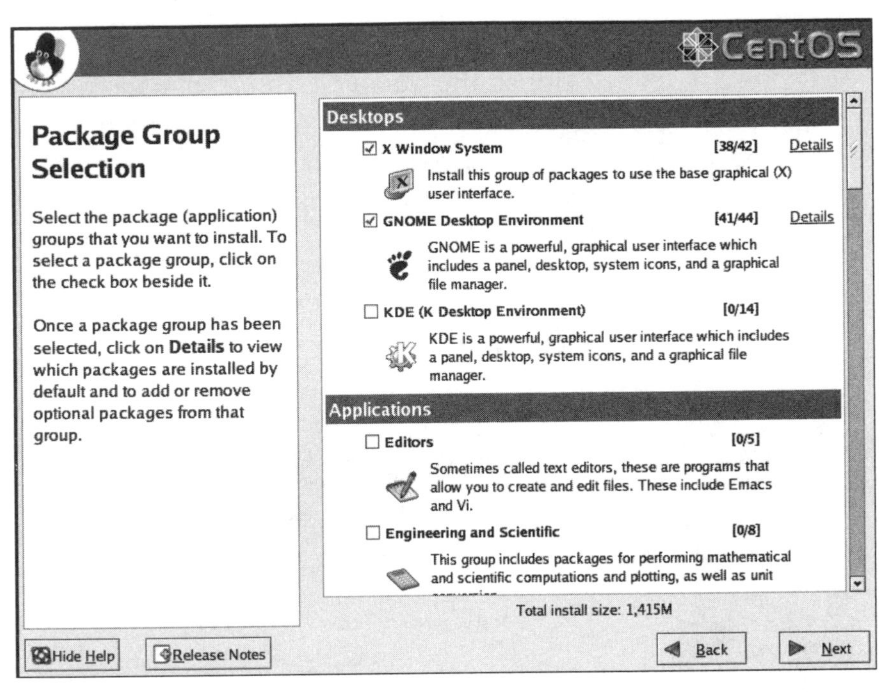

Figure 5.14: *Software Package Selection*

The following are offered as recommendations for minimal choices. Well, as nice as it would be to skip X-Windows (i.e. boot in terminal mode), the X-Windows environment is needed to run the Oracle installer, which is a Java based GUI (Graphical User Interface) product. So the first two choices for X-Windows and the Gnome Desktop are the bare minimums. From there, it all depends on user preference. Some people like to include an FTP server so that they can transfer files over to the client (e.g. the Oracle install image). And while that is a relatively easy and straightforward process, it nonetheless is very inefficient because the same data is being stored twice on the laptop's/notebook's limited disk space. Thus, it is often wise to install the Windows File Server, i.e. Samba. Samba will be selected for now and later the system will be set up to see the host's file system.

Towards the very end of the install process, the Linux installer will present what it thinks the default Display characteristics are (shown below in Figure 5.15). This is a very easy screen to ignore and rush through. But there are some real performance and usability implications here, so tale the time to make some wiser choices.

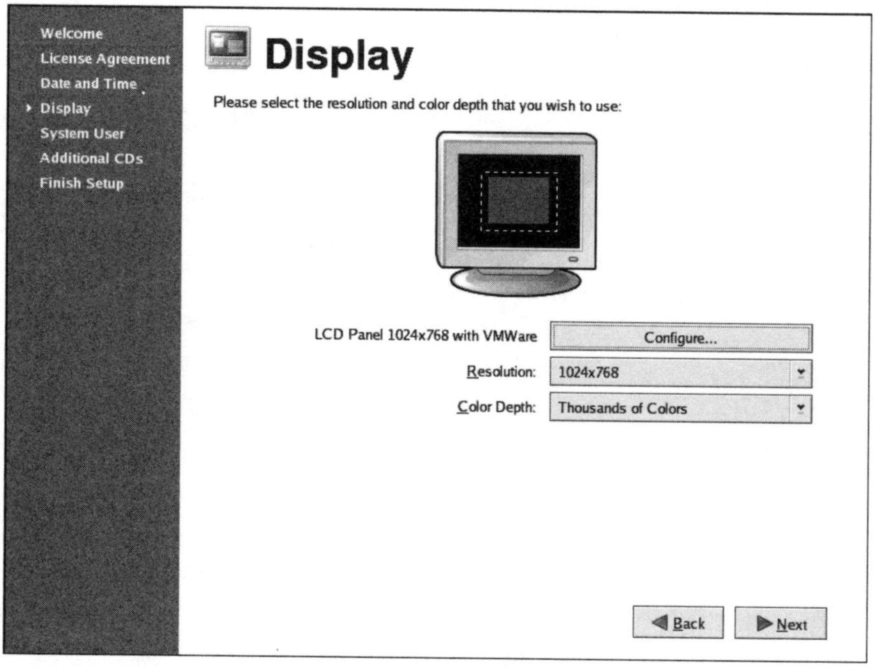

Welcome
License Agreement
Date and Time
Display
System User
Additional CDs
Finish Setup

Display

Please select the resolution and color depth that you wish to use:

LCD Panel 1024x768 with VMWare — Configure...
Resolution: 1024x768
Color Depth: Thousands of Colors

Back Next

Figure 5.15: *Display Characteristics Screen*

The default display type most often comes up as 800x600. And while that is an efficient setting, with today's higher display resolution capabilities, 1024x768 is a reasonable choice that balances efficiency with usability. As for the color depth, thousands of colors will more than suffice. Millions of colors is not necessary, especially if the GUI on the client is not being used other than to run the Oracle installer and occasionally show that Linux is running under the covers. Besides, it is quite possible that the exact same concession has already been made on the Windows display settings. It does not really make sense to tell Windows to restrict its color palette and then turn around and tell one of its applications (i.e. VMware) to use more than the operating system permits. The display characteristics discussion also nicely segues into the next topic.

The VMware client operating system and GUI run inside a virtual container created on the host operating system. As such, there are some tools, like highly specialized drivers, that the client operating system and GUI can use to more efficiently communicate with the host container. Those VMware tools need to be installed manually and for each client operating system. This is not an automatic step and is often forgotten. Note in the lower left corner of the screen snapshot shown in Figure 5.16 that VMware shows that this situation exists with a warning sign prominently displayed whenever the focus is the VMware host's main window.

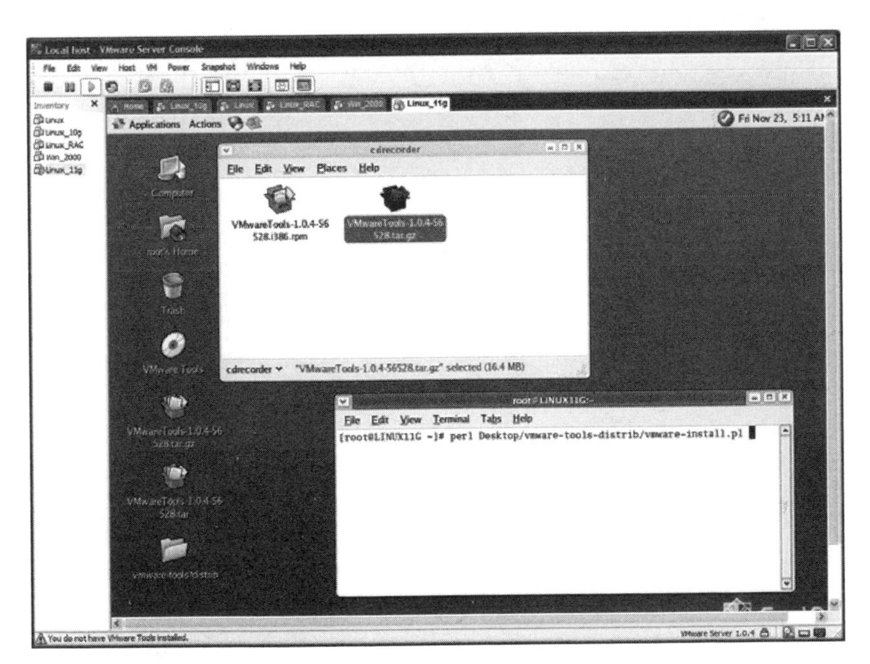

Figure 5.16: *VMware Tools Warning Sign*

However, it is very easy to address. Under the VM menu option on the VMware server's main menu, there is a choice for Install VMware Tools. Once selected, this will result in the VMware Tools showing up on the Linux desktop. Now open the VMware Tools CD by double clicking on it. There are two ways in which to install these tools. First, right-click on the .rpm file and select Open with Install Packages. However, there are times when this approach will seem to work, yet the warning message will remain. So the second and often more reliable method is to drag the zip file onto the desktop, unzip it, untar it, and then run the Perl script installation like shown in the command window in Figure 5.16.

Having gotten pretty close to having an optimal Linux operating system install as the VMware client, it is time to install Oracle. The next issue to address is how to make that Oracle software installation available to the Linux client. There are four methods generally available:

- Neither host nor client has the software, so mount a DVD with the Oracle install image on the Linux client. This option would be considered the normal way.
- Host has a copy of the Oracle install image, so FTP over a copy to the Linux client. This is wasteful since it doubles the cost of disk space.
- Host has a copy of the Oracle install image, so use Samba to make those files available from Windows host to Linux client
- Neither host nor client has the software, so mount a DVD or flash drive with the Oracle install image on the Windows host and use Samba to make that device available to Linux client

Using Samba often makes good sense since it makes file transfers so seamless and easy. A DBA will often have a collection of SQL scripts on their Windows hosts that they would like to be able to run from the Linux client. Option #3 will be the choice for this example.

Note that it is possible to "kill two birds with one stone" during this step since the Samba mount point entry goes in the /etc/fstab file – which is the exact same file that needs to be modified for the *",noatime"* file system optimization that was covered in Chapter 4. Figure 5.17 shows the recommended changes to the /etc/fstab file. The first two lines add *",noatime"* to the /boot and / mount points. The last line adds a Samba mount point for the host's C\: drive, thereby making it accessible from the Linux client.

```
root@LINUX:~
File  Edit  View  Terminal  Tabs  Help
[root@LINUX ~]# cat /etc/fstab
LABEL=/                /                   ext3,noatime  defaults                         1 1
LABEL=/boot            /boot               ext3,noatime  defaults                         1 2
none                   /dev/pts            devpts        gid=5,mode=620                   0 0
none                   /dev/shm            tmpfs         defaults                         0 0
none                   /proc               proc          defaults                         0 0
none                   /sys                sysfs         defaults                         0 0
LABEL=SWAP-sda2        swap                swap          defaults                         0 0
/dev/hdc               /media/cdrecorder   auto          pamconsole,exec,noauto,managed   0 0
/dev/fd0               /media/floppy       auto          pamconsole,exec,noauto,managed   0 0
//192.168.100.1/c$ /home/c_drive           smbfs         username=bert,password=bert,ro   0 0
[root@LINUX ~]#
```

Figure 5.17: *Recommended Changes to /etc/fstab File*

Finally, Linux services need to be configured to auto start when the client virtual machine is booted. While it is not wise to turn off anything necessary, it is also not advisable to autorun anything that is unnecessary. For example, anything that would be classified as purely overhead for demo purposes, such as printing. There are three ways to modify the services started:

- Services Management GUI (main menu: Applications->System Settings->Server Settings->Services)
- Command Line
  - chkconfig –level 5 service_name off
  - chkconfig –del service_name

Note: Using the *"–del"* version of the chkconfig command will disable that service across all run levels. That may be preferable since the DBA might want to switch the Linux run level to non-GUI after Oracle has been installed and configured. However, X-Windows GUI does not seem to place that high a load on the system, so it is generally a personal preference these days. But if after installing Oracle, that final system tweak can be accomplished through one of the following:

- Execute command: init run_level
- Edit the /etc/inittab file to set the run level

Here are some services that are not really needed for simple demo purposes:

- anacron (unless scheduling cron jobs)
- apmd
- atd (unless using the *"at"* command)
- crond (unless scheduling cron jobs)
- cups
- cups-config rsh
- haldaemon
- isdn
- kudzu
- lvm2-monitor (unless using the logical volume manager)
- mdmonitor

- netfs
- nfslock
- openibd
- pcmcia
- rawdevices (unless using Oracle with raw devices)
- sendmail
- smartd

The goal here is not to reduce the effectiveness of the Linux client, but merely to lighten its load for things that are not needed to run Oracle or give basic demos. If everything is done right, the end result will be minimal services auto-started as shown below in Figure 5.18):

```
root@LINUX:~
File Edit View Terminal Tabs Help
[root@LINUX ~]# chkconfig --list | grep '0:.*5:on.*' | sort
autofs          0:off   1:off   2:off   3:on    4:on    5:on    6:off
cpuspeed        0:off   1:on    2:on    3:on    4:on    5:on    6:off
iptables        0:off   1:off   2:on    3:on    4:on    5:on    6:off
irqbalance      0:off   1:off   2:off   3:on    4:on    5:on    6:off
messagebus      0:off   1:off   2:off   3:on    4:on    5:on    6:off
microcode_ctl   0:off   1:off   2:on    3:on    4:on    5:on    6:off
network         0:off   1:off   2:on    3:on    4:on    5:on    6:off
portmap         0:off   1:off   2:off   3:on    4:on    5:on    6:off
rawdevices      0:off   1:off   2:off   3:on    4:on    5:on    6:off
readahead       0:off   1:off   2:off   3:on    4:off   5:on    6:off
readahead_early 0:off   1:off   2:off   3:on    4:off   5:on    6:off
rpcgssd         0:off   1:off   2:off   3:on    4:on    5:on    6:off
rpcidmapd       0:off   1:off   2:off   3:on    4:on    5:on    6:off
sshd            0:off   1:off   2:on    3:on    4:on    5:on    6:off
syslog          0:off   1:off   2:on    3:on    4:on    5:on    6:off
sysstat         0:off   1:on    2:on    3:on    4:on    5:on    6:off
vmware-tools    0:off   1:off   2:on    3:on    4:off   5:on    6:off
vsftpd          0:off   1:off   2:off   3:off   4:off   5:on    6:off
xfs             0:off   1:off   2:on    3:on    4:on    5:on    6:off
xinetd          0:off   1:off   2:off   3:on    4:on    5:on    6:off
[root@LINUX ~]#
```

Figure 5.18: *Minimal Services in Auto-Start*

At this point, an optimal Linux operating system install exists as the VMware client and it is ready for installing Oracle. The only problem that might occur is that the Linux install may not have, by default, installed the *"libaio"* packages necessary for Oracle to do asynchronous I/O. This can always be installed manually anytime.

Oracle 11g Software Install

The Oracle Installer is a Java based GUI that is pretty straightforward. Consequently, there will not be a lot of elaboration offered along the way, but rather areas where some very conscious decisions will need to be made will be pointed out. First, it is highly recommend that the Advanced Installation option be chosen off the first page as shown in Figure 5.19. The optimal results will not be achieved via a default starter database and it will be necessary to make other decisions along the way.

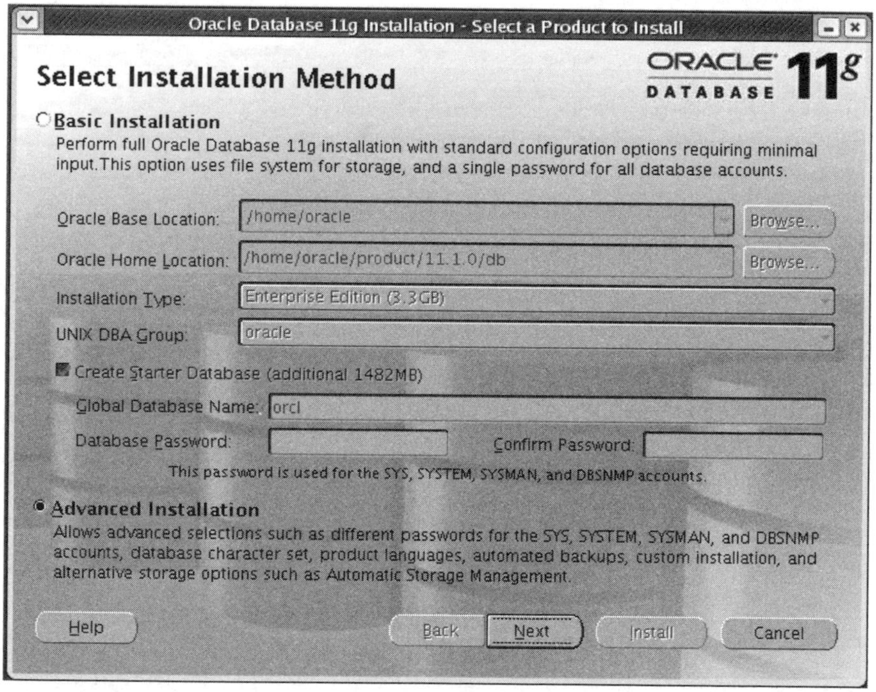

Figure 5.19: *Advanced Installation Option in Oracle 11g*

As installation progresses, the installer will offer an option to install either the "Enterprise Edition" (i.e. the whole enchilada) or custom. While typically Enterprise Edition is chosen, if the goal is a truly bare minimum installation, then choose custom install and deselect the following as appropriate for individual demo needs:

- Oracle Advanced Security
- Oracle Spatial
- Oracle OLAP
- Oracle Data Mining RDBMS Files
- Oracle Real Application Testing
- Oracle Programmer

Even though the XML Development Kit may not be desired, it is a mandatory component that must be installed. When later asked about creating a database, choose "Install Database Software Only" for now.

Create the Demo Database

The Oracle Database Configuration Assistant (DBCA) is a Java based GUI that is also straightforward. Once again, there will not be a lot of elaboration offered along the way, but rather areas where some very conscious decisions will need to be made will be pointed out. This example assumes "Enterprise Edition" was chosen during the install. This means there may have more choices to make during the database creation process than if a minimalist installation of Oracle had been selected.

There lots of us who say "GUIs are bad, real DBAs run scripts." On the purely technical side, there was a time when many a DBA considered the only way to create a database was via their own handwritten SQL scripts. But over the years, the Oracle database has become so complex in terms of options that writing such scripts became inefficient. Fortunately at the very same time, the Database Configuration Assistant (DBCA) has become so good that handwritten scripts are rarely needed anymore, especially for RAC deployments, where DBCA is much quicker and better than most DBAs could ever aspire to be.

But now because of this very factor – that DBCA is generally good enough for creating databases – it has been easy to miss the fact that the database software has many more options that require deliberate decisions. This means that the DBA can no longer start up DBCA to create a database and then mindlessly press the "Next" button until it starts working. That may have been acceptable and safe back with 8i, but 11g is definitely a different animal. The DBA should carefully navigate the DBCA screens and options and feel free to choose to disable or change significant items if deploying Oracle on a notebook or desktop with limited resources.

Here are just a few examples of why it is strongly recommended to cautiously navigate and select from DBCA. Many items listed below are generally not really needed all the time or very conducive to use on simple non-production or demo systems with limited I/O bandwidth:

Important

- 11g now defaults to auditing turned on and stored in the database
- DBCA defaults to installing Java Virtual Machine and XML DB
- DB multi file read count seems to default to a much higher value
- File system I/O options defaults to NONE – wish it would just choose SETALL
- Job queue processes now defaults to 1000 instead of 10 – that is a very big change

- There are more pre-supplied Oracle jobs to actually do self-maintenance
- Max dump file size still defaults to UNLIMITED – never a good choice for PCs
- XML DB Events default to ENABLED since default is now to install XML DB
- Recycle BIN still defaults to ON –and thus people potentially collect junk
- SGA now has some additional new areas: Results Cache, Function Cache, etc.

The above should be sufficient for most people to see that when creating an Oracle database on a smaller machine, like a notebook, it is clearly best not to just blindly accept the DBCA defaults anymore. When done properly, it is possible to run 10g, 11g and a two node 10g RAC cluster all on a Windows XP notebook without any major headaches. Even when running them all concurrently!

When running DBCA, please make sure to pick Custom Database as shown in Figure 5.20. The reason is very simple – in order to be able to change redo log and data file size allocations, then the custom option must be selected. Otherwise, DBCA blindly copies over some pre-existing files of a set size that usually is not too good. Knowledgeable DBAs can pick better, so choose custom.

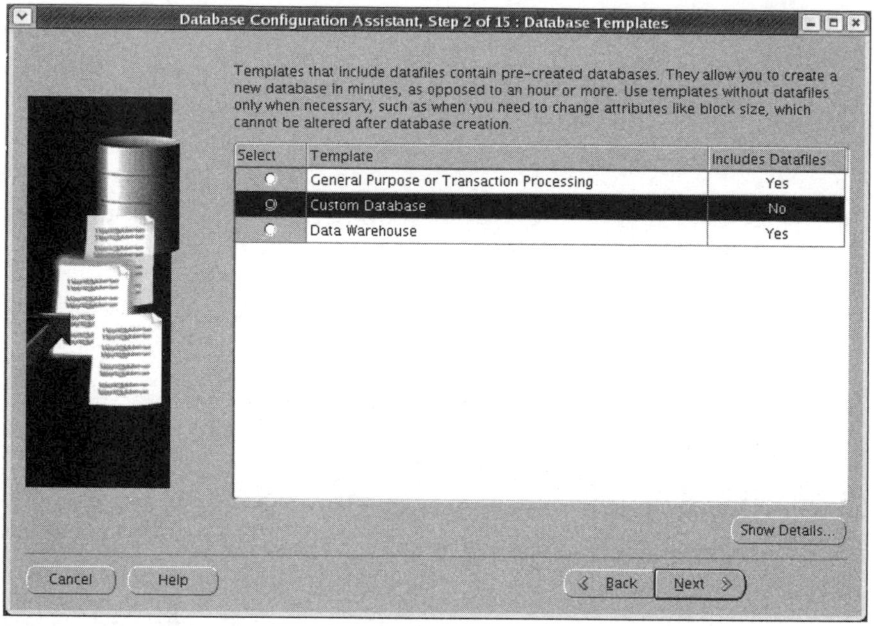

Figure 5.20: *Database Configuration Screen*

Once step four is reached, there will be an option to enable or not enable the Oracle Enterprise Manager (OEM). Since this author works for Quest Software and most often needs to demo Quest's tools and usually not Oracle's, it is possible to forgo installing OEM. That saves both disk space for the extra data dictionary and SYSAUX tablespace allocations. Plus, it installs less Linux background processes to support that database. This second savings is probably more worthwhile if OEM is not needed.

At step six there will be three options for the storage mechanism for Oracle database files: file system, ASM, or raw devices. As was pointed out in Chapter 4, some performance gains can be realized on the I/Os via either ASM or RAW devices. But both options add additional levels of complexities as well (e.g. ASM means there are two instances running). The file system option is generally recommended for simplicity and overall ease of space management.

On step eight as shown in Figure 5.21, there will be to decision options: flash recovery and archiving. While these probably make good sense in production and/or test systems, for development or demo databases it is possible to do without these overheads. So for the laptop/notebook demo setup example, no has been selected for each.

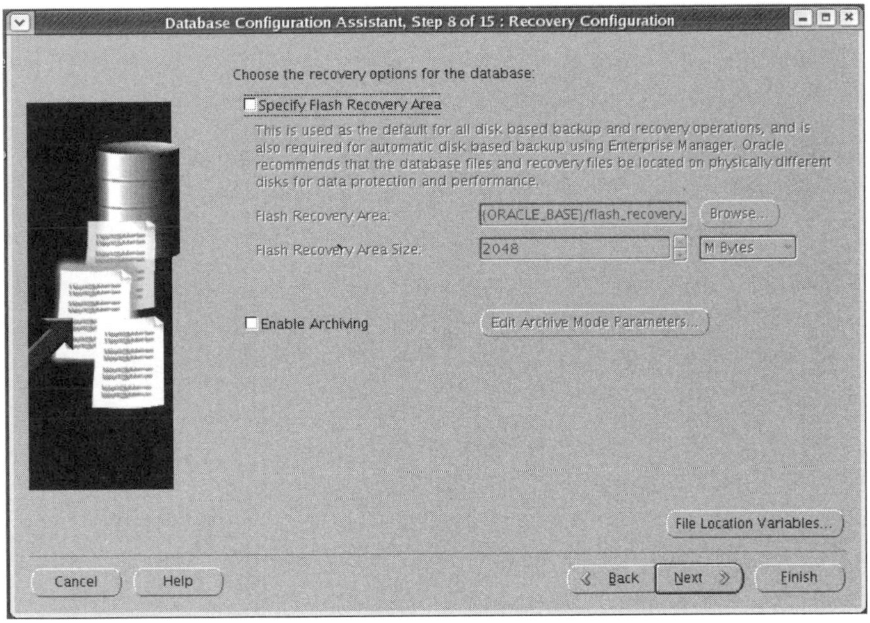

Figure 5.21: *Recovery Configuration Screen*

At step nine, shown in Figure 5.22, there are some very important options that can greatly reduce the data dictionary size, significantly reduce SYSTEM and SYSAUX tablespace needs, plus radically reduce the time it takes to actually run the script to create the database -sometimes by a factor of two or more. Not to mention that the resulting database will require less overhead for background processes and significantly less I/O with archiving turned off. Again, for demos this is typically not a problem or bad choice. But this decision will be determined by need. For most simplistic demo purposes, all these options can be disabled as well as the Standard Database Components for Oracle JVM, Oracle XML DB, Oracle Multi-Media, and Oracle Application Express. While DBCA will give a warning that XML DB is generally necessary for other pre-installed packages, it is not likely that disabling this choice with any ill effects. As before, this is a personal decision.

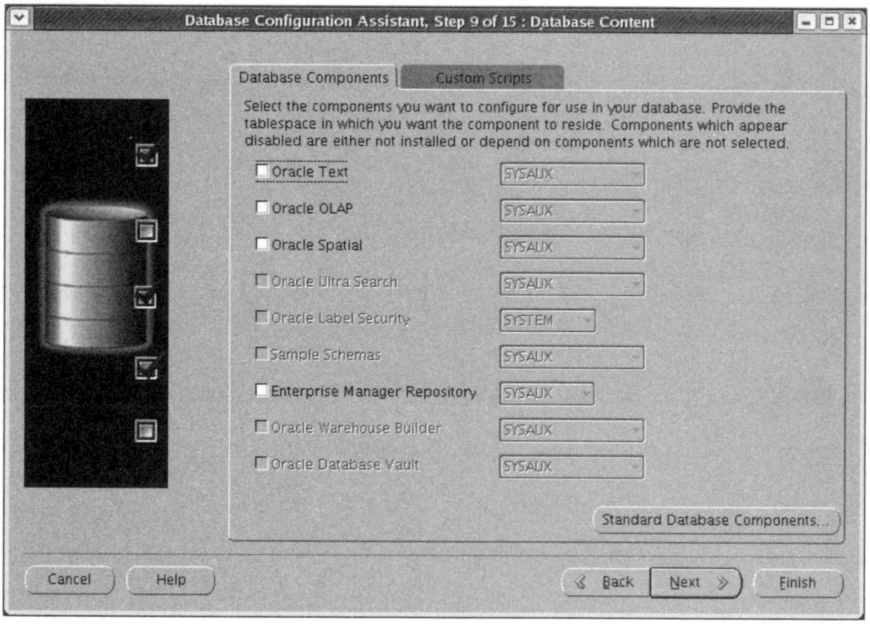

Figure 5.22: *Step 9 in Database Configuration Assistant*

Step ten probably presents some familiar decision points. There are three recommendations here. First, do not allocate more than 40% of the system memory to Oracle. Remember that the goal here is to do a minimal install to get 11g running on a single CPU system with just 1 GB of memory. Second, on the sizing tab, choose a block size of 4K and no more than 300 processes. And third, open the All Initialization Parameters window and choose the option for Show Advanced Parameters – making sure to visit and set values such as:

- *auditing_trail* = NONE
- *cursor_sharing* = SIMILAR
- *cursor_space_for_time* = TRUE
- *db_file_multiblock_read_count* = 2
- *filesystemio_options* = SETALL
- *job_queue_processes* = 20
- *max_dump_file_size* = 10M
- *xml_db_events* = DISABLE

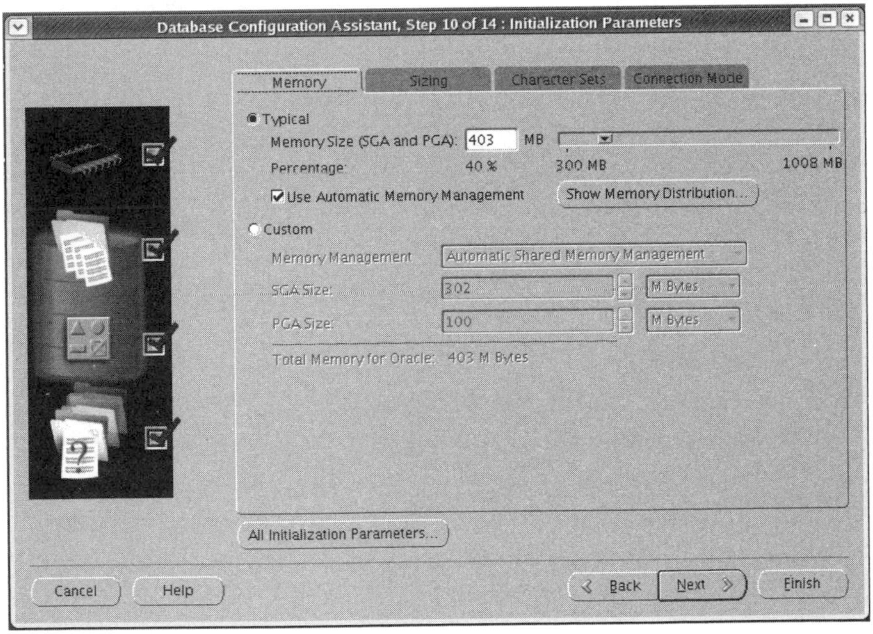

Figure 5.23: *Recommended Settings for Initialization Parameters*

That leaves just one key step to complete the database creation process: defining all the sizes and database storage parameters for the default tablespaces created. This is the one key step that will not occur if anything other than a custom database creation is selected. There are many parameters here worth setting, as the table below details:

TABLESPACE	BIGFILE	ALLOCATION	LOGGING	SIZE	AUTO EXTEND
SYSAUX	YES	Uniform – 1M	NO	200M	20M
SYSTEM	YES	Uniform – 1M	NO	300M	20M
TEMP	YES	Uniform – 1M		200M	20M
UNDOTBS1	YES			200M	10M
USERS	YES	Uniform – 1M	NO	200M	10M

Table 5.1: *Default Tablespace Sizes and Database Storage Parameters*

Note that setting all the above requires visiting each tablespace and data file in the tree and selecting both the general and storage tab for each. Use caution here because much of the above cannot easily be changed once the database has been created.

DB Auto-Start

Naturally, the easiest option will be make it so that the virtual machine running the Linux client operating system and the Oracle database always auto-starts to keep the demo process easy. That requires just three easy steps shown below. Take note that for RAC setups this script will become a lot more complex.

1. Create auto start script /etc/init.d directory/dbstart_auto.sh

```
ORACLE_HOME=/home/oracle/product/10.2.0/db
export ORACLE_HOME
su - oracle -c "$ORACLE_HOME/bin/lsnrctl start" > /dev/null
su - oracle -c "$ORACLE_HOME/bin/dbstart" > /dev/null
```

2. Create auto stop script /etc/init.d directory/dbshut_auto.sh

```
ORACLE_HOME=/home/oracle/product/10.2.0/db
export ORACLE_HOME
su - oracle -c "$ORACLE_HOME/bin/lsnrctl stop" > /dev/null
su - oracle -c "$ORACLE_HOME/bin/dbshut" > /dev/null
```

3. Then execute the following commands to set it all up

```
ln -sf  /etc/init.d/dbshut_auto.sh   /etc/rc0.d/K10dbshut
ln -sf  /etc/init.d/dbshut_auto.sh   /etc/rc6.d/K10dbshut
ln -sf  /etc/init.d/dbstart_auto.sh  /etc/rc2.d/S99dbstart
ln -sf  /etc/init.d/dbstart_auto.sh  /etc/rc5.d/S99dbstart
```

Conclusion

In this chapter, an ideal minimal Oracle installation and database creation was created for the purpose of basic demos on hardware with limited capabilities (e.g. laptops and notebooks). While the process itself was not that hard, many of the steps are recommendations for items to turn off or reduce from their defaults and which are often very easily missed in the haste to simply press Next repeatedly to complete the installation and database creation as quickly as possible.

The next chapter will explore this same scenario for a demo machine running RAC.

Pseudo RAC Setup

CHAPTER

"Miss Jones, we need Oracle RAC. Please find out what RAC is!"

Overview

Much like the last chapter, this chapter will highlight the recipe for creating an Oracle database VMware *golden image*. Only this time it will be for what can be referred to as a *pseudo-RAC* setup. That is a RAC (Resolved Acceleration Control) cluster running on just a single node but appearing to the outside world as a true RAC environment. And yes, this is not a setup that Oracle actually intends people to use and which they really do not support; nonetheless, it is often a highly desirable setup for demo purposes. For those who need to demo RAC or RAC related products while traveling or those who simply want to create a dirt cheap RAC playground for learning and/or experimentation, this recipe will more than suffice.

For example, to demo Quest Software's outstanding diagnostic tool Spotlight for RAC shown in Figure 6.1 on a notebook while at a customer site, the Oracle side of the equation needs to appear like a true RAC environment. In this case, a single notebook is running two Oracle RAC instances that are hosted by one virtual machine which is running one instance of Linux. So it is possible to create and run such a pseudo-RAC environment in just 1 GB of memory and 20 GB of disk space. Any notebook with, say, a dual core processor, 2 GB of memory and a 60 GB or larger disk drive can be effectively pressed into such service.

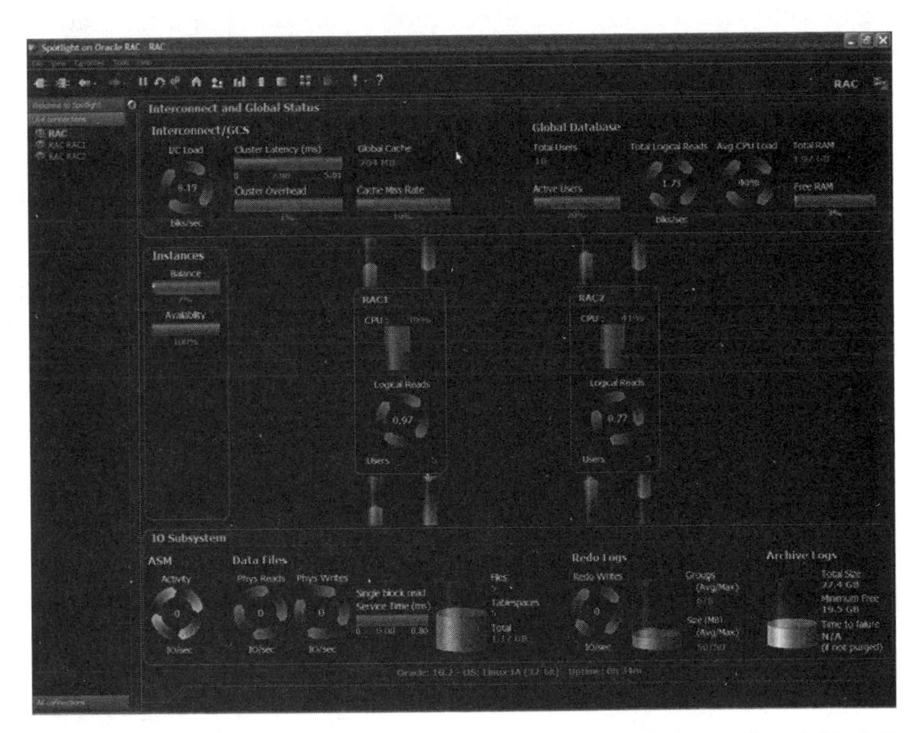

Figure 6.1: *Quest Software Diagnostic Tool – Spotlight on Oracle RAC*

So what are the benefits to such a setup? From the database or RAC perspective, there are none. But from the user's perspective, there are many, including:

- Truly portable RAC environment
- Requires minimal memory and disk space
- Could easily be scaled for more RAC instances
- Does NOT require expensive SAN for shared storage

And while all these points make this setup interesting, it is quite often the final bullet that gets most peoples' attention. But it cannot be stressed enough that this configuration is **not recommended** for anything other than limited uses and never ever for production or even testing environments. For that, the next chapter might hold a solution that can minimally address those environments' extended needs. So only use this type of configuration where appropriate.

Preparation

Every single step will not be repeated in this recipe as that would greatly inflate what is already going to be a long chapter. Instead, the information presented will show the steps that differ from the first recipe. Therefore, a thorough perusal of the previous chapter is highly recommended before proceeding. This chapter will only highlight the points along the way where something different needs to be done, and will assume that all the other steps have already been applied at their appropriate points along the way.

Note that in the last chapter, an Oracle 11g database setup was created. Since 11g is still under a year old – and many surveys show that about 35% of the people are on 9i with plans to upgrade now to 10g, and another 35% are on 10g already with no plans to upgrade yet to 11g – that version Oracle 10g is going to be used in this chapter is still quite relevant for a majority of the people. So what does this mean in terms of work to be performed?

If a VMware *golden image* exists with just the base Linux install, then it is best to start with that. If not, then it is best to start over and create such an image now. Because, as one might guess, the same dilemma will be faced in the next chapter and for any future efforts, so might as well bite the bullet now and build a base Linux VMware *golden image* from which to work. Such an image should zip up to well under 1 GB and thus be both useful and small enough to fit on either a DVD or USB flash drive. That way, it is handy whenever it is needed.

On the other hand, to take a path of least resistance right now, reuse the VMware image from the last chapter. This example will go through the steps for installing a second Oracle home if 10g will be used or the existing 11g Oracle home that was created in the prior chapter can be used. The only difference will be that some of the 10g screen snapshots shown in this chapter will differ slightly from those that will be encountered with 11g but the steps are essentially the same. Using the existing installation will save lots of work!

One final note worth mention – it is probably worthwhile to zip up the directories for each of these *golden image* recipes/projects once they are completed because each represents an effective use case that requires significant effort to reconstruct. This author actually has an entire 500 GB network drive allocated for keeping only an ever growing library of VMware images – time is money!

VMware Host Settings

There is only one additional requirement this time around – the host needs to provide two network cards to virtual machines: one for the Oracle public network and one for the Oracle private network, i.e. the RAC interconnect. Hence, the host should be configured as shown in Figure 6.2. Do not be confused by the terminology here. The VMware network settings are both *Host-only*, which simply means that they cannot see the outside world. But they can see everything within that host including both the Oracle public and private networks. To make this setup available to other PCs, open up the VMnet1 network setting.

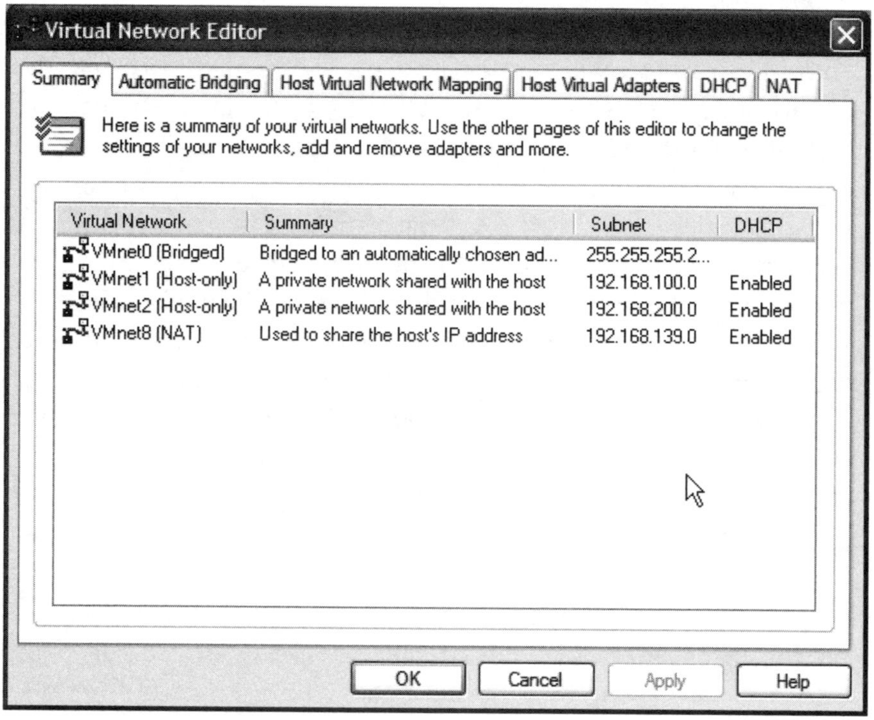

Figure 6.2: *Host Configuration Screen*

Note that the only difference between VMnet1 and VMnet2 are the assigned IP addresses. The 192.168.100.xxx range is allocated for the Oracle public network, and 192.168.200.xxx range for the Oracle private network. The following changes should be made to the hosts file. The new entries are in bold:

```
# Laptop/Notebook Demo HOSTS file
#
127.0.0.1                    localhost
192.168.100.101     linux
192.168.100.102     linux_10g
192.168.100.103     linux_11g
192.168.100.104     linux_rac
192.168.200.104     linux_rac-priv
192.168.100.105     linux_rac-vip
```

Note that last new entry above for the Oracle virtual IP address, which is not represented in the VMware host network settings. Oracle will create a special network adapter itself on the VMware client operating system to handle load balancing and fault tolerance. This step is covered in more detail later in this chapter. Since the entire RAC cluster is really all on one node, the *linux_rac* alias could be used. But in an effort to keep this setup as realistic as possible, use the virtual IP address of *linux_rac-vip* just like any other normal RAC configuration.

Virtual Machine Setup

Two key modifications need to be made to the virtual machine setup as shown in Figure 6.3. Both changes are very easy and should take only a moment to complete. These changes can be easily made to an existing VMware image in case pre-existing VMware *golden image* is being used.

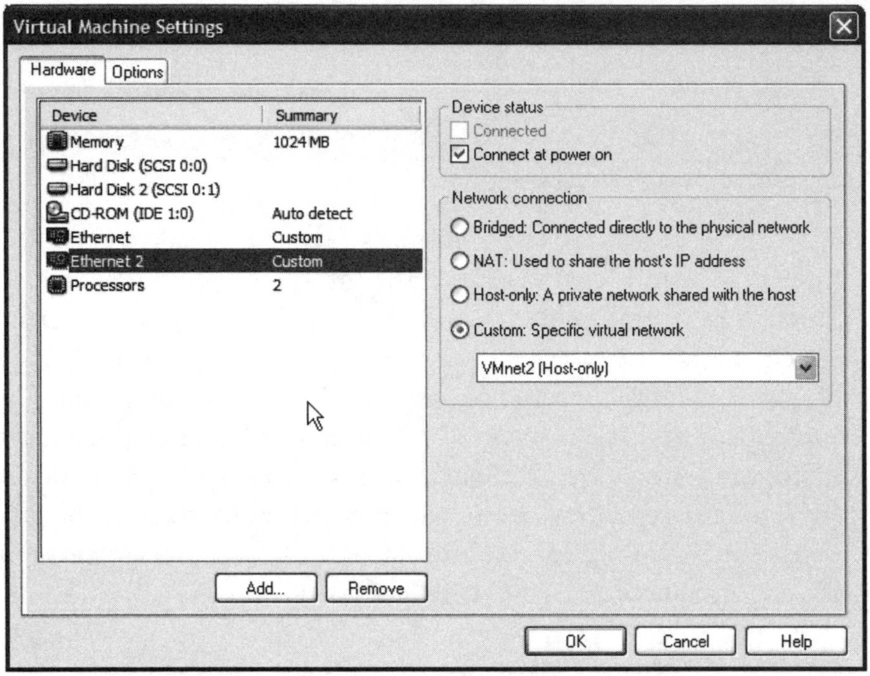

Figure 6.3: *Virtual Machine Setup Modifications*

First, a second hard disk device needs to be added to host the shared file system for the RAC cluster. For this example, Hard Disk 2 has been added and 10 GB has been allocated to it. That is going to house the Oracle Cluster File System, or ocfs2. There are numerous other options not covered here:

- Allocate the second disk, but use Oracle ASM to manage the shared storage device. ASM will be used in the next chapter when doing a true multi-node RAC setup.
- Not allocate second disk, use Linux loop back devices to create the ocfs2 file system within the existing ext3 Linux file system
- Not allocate second disk, use Linux loop back devices to create raw devices to then allocate to ASM to manage as if real disks

- Allocate the second disk, but use a Linux clustered file system such as Open GFS, Red Hat GFS, Veritas Storage Foundation CFS, Poly Serve Matrix Server , IBM General Parallel File System, SGI XFS for Linux, HP Storage Works Scalable File Share, Sun Lustre File System, Sun SAM-QFS, etc.
- Allocate the second disk, but use VMware VMFS – a high performance cluster file system optimized for virtual machines

Of those choices, the first three alternatives could easily be used instead of the choice to allocate a second drive and use Oracle's ocfs2. And for simple demo, experimentation or playground type purposes, any of them will suffice without undo expense or difficulty. However, for testing and production purposes, only the first and final two choices make sense. Since ASM is free, readily supported and preferred for RAC setups, and being used by over 60% of new RAC deployments, it makes a good enough choice for demo purposes.

Next, a second Ethernet network card will need to be added based off VMnet2, which was defined in the prior step. This will be used by the RAC instances as the Oracle private network or interconnect. There are two important reasons for doing this. First, doing so most closely approximates a true RAC environment. Secondly, the RAC interconnect is often the bottleneck in overall maximum performance. So having it on a separate network provides better ability to monitor and diagnose such RAC interconnect issues if they occur.

Client Operating System

As with the virtual machine setup, there are just two critical modifications that need to be made during the operating system install. There are also a host of additional steps necessary to support ocfs2 and other RAC prerequisites, which will be covered now.

The first change during the OS install is to create a second disk device (/dev/sdb) as shown below in Figure 6.4 based off the second VMware hard disk device, which is Hard Disk 2 from the prior section. A file system does not need to be created on it yet – that will be accomplished later. For now, the OS needs to recognize and know about it.

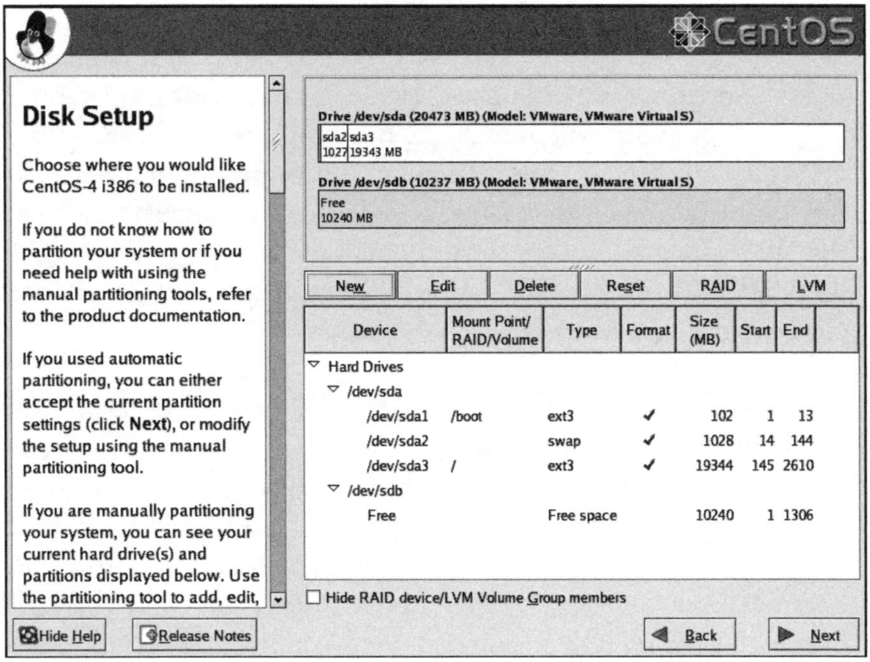

Figure 6.4: *Creating a Second Disk Device*

The second change during the OS install is to configure a second Ethernet network device, eth1, for the Oracle private network or interconnect (Figure 6.5). Although the assigned IP addresses may look very similar, note that one is on subnet 100 and the other on subnet 200. This is a very easy item to miss which can have drastic ramifications, such as the RAC cluster services failing to start or otherwise communicate. So take some time on this screen and make sure these settings and the hosts' file entries match.

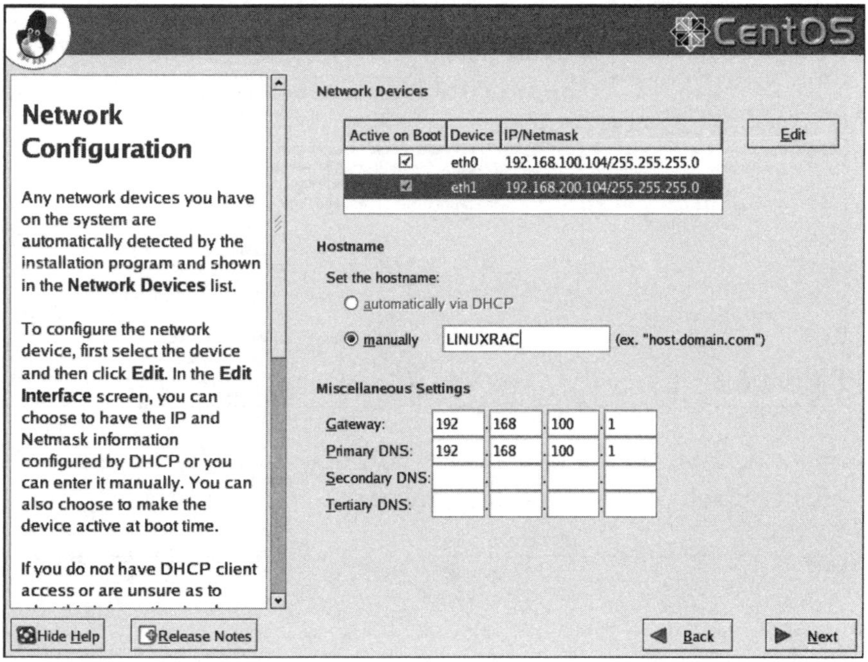

CentOS

Network Configuration

Any network devices you have on the system are automatically detected by the installation program and shown in the **Network Devices** list.

To configure the network device, first select the device and then click **Edit**. In the **Edit Interface** screen, you can choose to have the IP and Netmask information configured by DHCP or you can enter it manually. You can also choose to make the device active at boot time.

If you do not have DHCP client access or are unsure as to

Network Devices

Active on Boot	Device	IP/Netmask
☑	eth0	192.168.100.104/255.255.255.0
☑	eth1	192.168.200.104/255.255.255.0

Edit

Hostname

Set the hostname:

○ automatically via DHCP

◉ manually LINUXRAC (ex. "host.domain.com")

Miscellaneous Settings

Gateway:	192	168	100	1
Primary DNS:	192	168	100	1
Secondary DNS:				
Tertiary DNS:				

Hide Help | Release Notes | Back | Next

Figure 6.5: *Configuring Second Ethernet Network Device*

Once the operating system install is complete and all the other operating system steps from the prior chapter have been done, there are still a few remaining issues to address before moving on to the Oracle software install step.

First, the Oracle Cluster File System Linux kernel packages that match the Linux kernel version need to be installed. So issue the "uname –r" command as shown in Figure 6.6 to verify the Linux kernel version, then merely obtain and install those ocfs2 packages. The root user must be used to install packages.

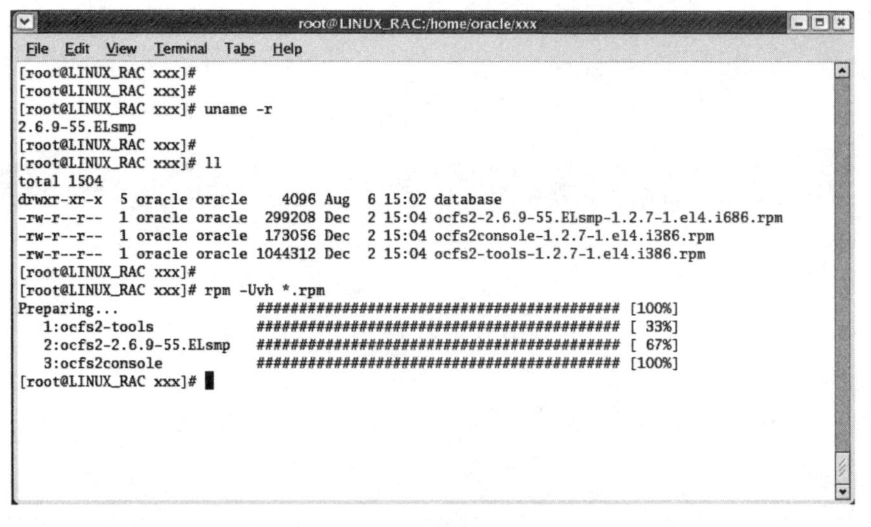

Figure 6.6: *Verifying Linux Kernel Version*

Second, run the ocfs2console command, GUI, to initiate the cluster stack services and to configure the cluster node.

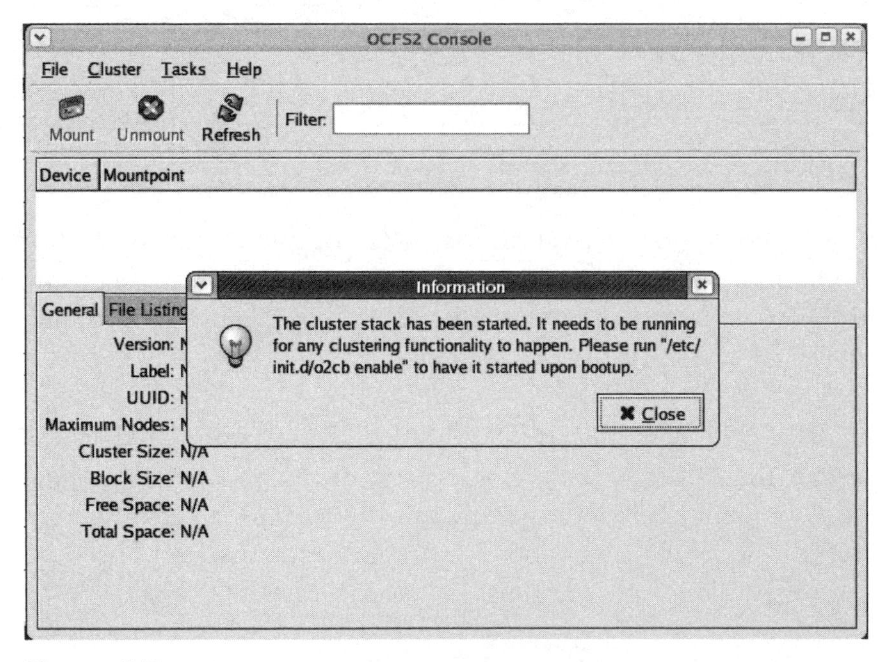

Figure 6.7: *Cluster Stack Services Screen*

To make sure that these cluster services autostart on reboot, the ocfs2console instructs the user to run the /etc/init.d/o2cd enable command. This is a critical step that is sometimes easy to skip over with devastating results, i.e. the cluster file system will not be accessible after reboot since the necessary prerequisite cluster services will not be running. So please do not skip this step.

Next, choose the Main Menu → Cluster → Configure Nodes options to launch the screen shown in Figure 6.8. Add the network alias and IP address here. The port can be permitted to default. This is all for the ocfs2console utility.

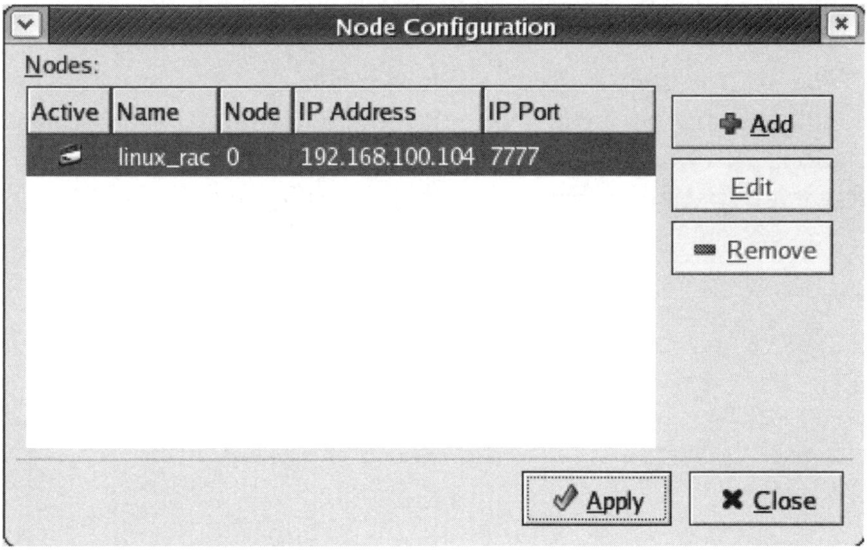

Figure 6.8: *Adding Network Alias and IP Address*

There are just three more steps to go to complete the operating system level installation and configuration:

- Configure the cluster services (optional step)
- Format the cluster file system on /dev/sdb

- Mount and/or auto-mount the ocfs2 file system

This first step is optional. However, it is shown here since, for some real-world scenarios, this step may be critical (such as in the next chapter). This is accomplished by taking the ocfs2 file system offline and unloading its packages, then running its configuration script. While it asks several questions, including one about the autostart on reboot, it is the *heartbeat* question that requires special attention. It is not uncommon on lower capacity systems or systems with inherent time lags (e.g. NAS or iSCSI) to require adjusting the heartbeat threshold higher. For such occasions it is often quite advisable to choose a value of 60 or higher. The default of 31 or lower may often result in nodes appearing to sporadically hang.

The second step is pretty straight forward - an ocfs2 file system still need to be created on the device (e.g. /dev/sdb) that was allocated during the operating system install for the shared disk storage space required by Oracle RAC (Figure 6.9).

```
root@LINUX_RAC:/home/oracle/xxx
File  Edit  View  Terminal  Tabs  Help
[root@LINUX_RAC xxx]# /etc/init.d/o2cb offline ocfs2
Stopping O2CB cluster ocfs2: OK
[root@LINUX_RAC xxx]#
[root@LINUX_RAC xxx]# /etc/init.d/o2cb unload
Unmounting ocfs2_dlmfs filesystem: OK
Unloading module "ocfs2_dlmfs": OK
Unmounting configfs filesystem: OK
Unloading module "configfs": OK
[root@LINUX_RAC xxx]#
[root@LINUX_RAC xxx]# /etc/init.d/o2cb configure
Configuring the O2CB driver.

This will configure the on-boot properties of the O2CB driver.
The following questions will determine whether the driver is loaded on
boot.  The current values will be shown in brackets ('[]').  Hitting
<ENTER> without typing an answer will keep that current value.  Ctrl-C
will abort.

Load O2CB driver on boot (y/n) [n]: y
Cluster to start on boot (Enter "none" to clear) [ocfs2]:
Specify heartbeat dead threshold (>=7) [31]:
Specify network idle timeout in ms (>=5000) [30000]:
Specify network keepalive delay in ms (>=1000) [2000]:
Specify network reconnect delay in ms (>=2000) [2000]:
Writing O2CB configuration: OK
Loading module "configfs": OK
Mounting configfs filesystem at /config: OK
Loading module "ocfs2_nodemanager": OK
Loading module "ocfs2_dlm": OK
Loading module "ocfs2_dlmfs": OK
Mounting ocfs2_dlmfs filesystem at /dlm: OK
Starting O2CB cluster ocfs2: OK
[root@LINUX_RAC xxx]#
```

Figure 6.9: *Screen showing creating an ocfs2 File System*

Then run the mkfs.ocfs command as shown below in Figure 6.10. The settings shown include a block size of 4K, a cluster size of 32K, and volume label of "oracrsfiles." The block size may seem a bit small by today's standards, but have faith for now and go with 4K. Chapter 9 will include an explanation where some more advanced tuning issues will be covered, especially as they relate to Oracle on virtual machines.

root@LINUX_RAC:/home/oracle/xxx

File Edit View Terminal Tabs Help

```
[root@LINUX_RAC xxx]#
[root@LINUX_RAC xxx]# mkfs.ocfs2 -b 4k -C 32k -N 4 -L oracrsfiles /dev/sdb
mkfs.ocfs2 1.2.7
Overwriting existing ocfs2 partition.
Proceed (y/N): y
Filesystem label=oracrsfiles
Block size=4096 (bits=12)
Cluster size=32768 (bits=15)
Volume size=10737418240 (327680 clusters) (2621440 blocks)
11 cluster groups (tail covers 5120 clusters, rest cover 32256 clusters)
Journal size=67108864
Initial number of node slots: 4
Creating bitmaps: done
Initializing superblock: done
Writing system files: done
Writing superblock: done
Writing backup superblock: 2 block(s)
Formatting Journals: done
Writing lost+found: done
mkfs.ocfs2 successful

[root@LINUX_RAC xxx]#
```

Figure 6.10: *Screen Showing Block Size*

Finally, create the ocfs2 file system mount point, change the owner to Oracle, set appropriate permissions, and mount the new ocfs2 file system to verify that everything was done correctly as shown in Figure 6.11.

root@LINUX_RAC:/

File Edit View Terminal Tabs Help

```
[root@LINUX_RAC /]#
[root@LINUX_RAC /]# mkdir /data
[root@LINUX_RAC /]# chown oracle:oracle /data
[root@LINUX_RAC /]# chmod 770 /data
[root@LINUX_RAC /]#
[root@LINUX_RAC /]# mount -t ocfs2 -o datavolume,nointr -L oracrsfiles /data
[root@LINUX_RAC /]#
[root@LINUX_RAC /]# cat /etc/fstab
LABEL=/          /                  ext3,noatime    defaults        1 1
LABEL=/boot      /boot              ext3,noatime    defaults        1 2
none             /dev/pts           devpts  gid=5,mode=620  0 0
none             /dev/shm           tmpfs   defaults        0 0
none             /proc              proc    defaults        0 0
none             /sys               sysfs   defaults        0 0
LABEL=SWAP-sda2  swap               swap    defaults        0 0
/dev/hdc         /media/cdrecorder  auto    pamconsole,exec,noauto,managed 0 0
/dev/fd0         /media/floppy      auto    pamconsole,exec,noauto,managed 0 0
LABEL=oracrsfiles /data             ocfs2   _netdev,datavolume,nointr 0 0
[root@LINUX_RAC /]#
[root@LINUX_RAC /]#
```

Figure 6.11: *Resolution of Proper Setup*

If that all works as expected, then an entry needs to be added to the /etc/fstab file to make sure that the new ocfs2 file system is auto mounted on boot. This completes the operating system level steps – on to the Oracle software.

Oracle 10G Software Install

The most notable change during this process is that two different Oracle software installs will have to be run: one for the cluster ware and then one for the database. These are two different downloads from the Oracle OTN site. So first obtain the Oracle clusterware install files, export ORACLE_HOME = /home/oracle/product/10.2.0/crs, and then run the clusterware's installer via the *runInstaller* script as shown in Figure 6.12. If everything has been done correctly to this point correctly, including setting the /etc/hosts file with all three mandatory RAC IP addresses, then the installer should recognize this as a legitimately clusterable node. If not, then backtrack and re-verify the prior steps done properly.

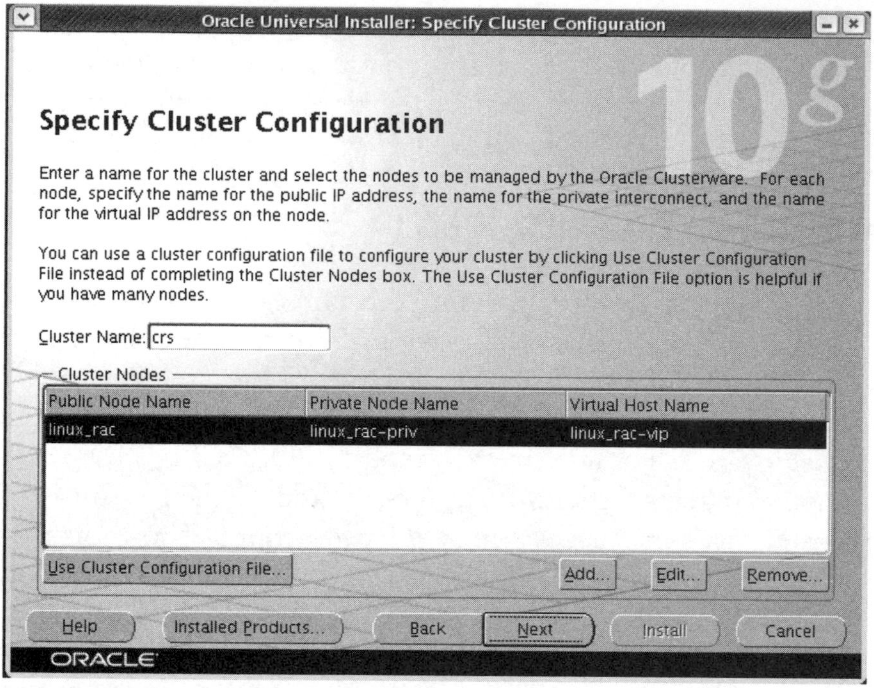

Figure 6.12: *Running Clusterware's Installer*

The first critical step will be the network interface screen shown in Figure 6.13. It is important to properly recognize both of the Oracle public and private network interfaces and with the proper interface type chosen. It is not uncommon for this screen to require manual adjustments to the interface type, as it often comes up with both being private. Just make sure to mark the correct one as public.

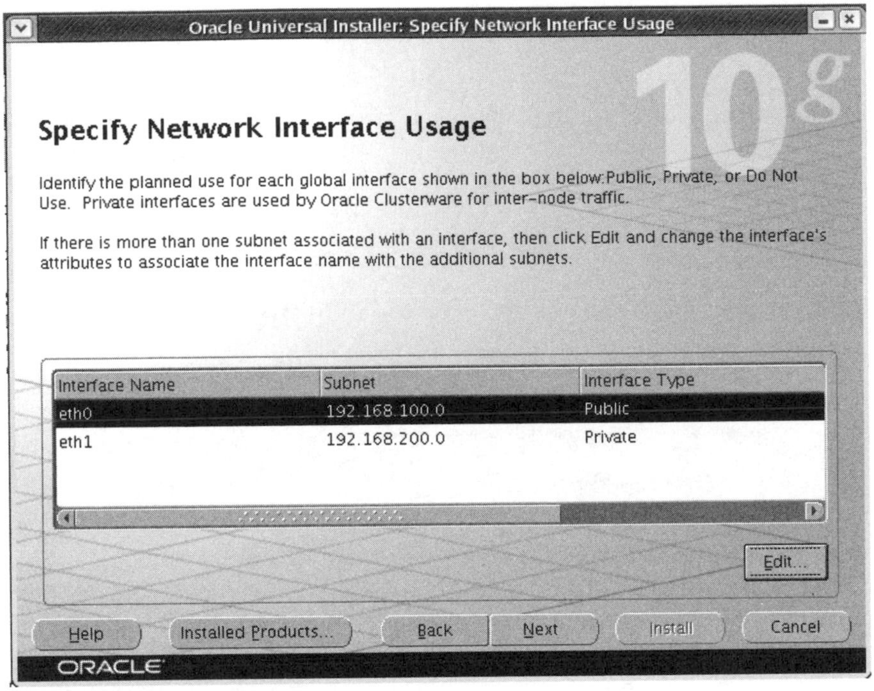

Figure 6.13: *Network Interface Screen*

The clusterware install will then ask for locations and redundancy nature for the cluster registry (OCR) and voting disk files which must reside on shared disk space. Note that as shown in the next two screen snapshots (Figures 14 and 15), easy names with no redundancy have been chosen to keep things simple, i.e. the choices are not really redundant because external implies it is being done externally – and in this case, it is just not being done at all. This installer will now create and format those files.

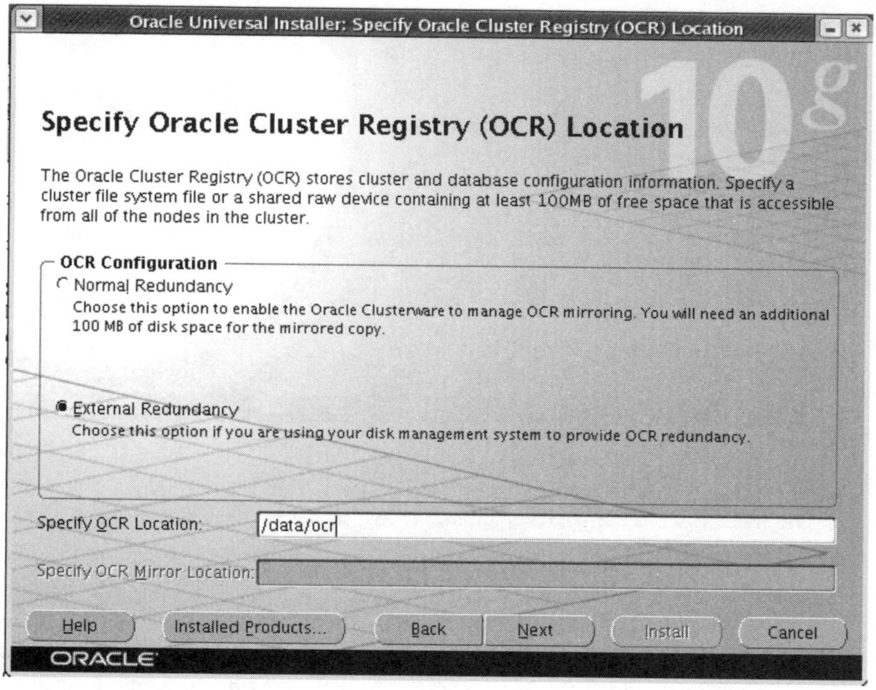

Oracle Universal Installer: Specify Oracle Cluster Registry (OCR) Location

Specify Oracle Cluster Registry (OCR) Location

The Oracle Cluster Registry (OCR) stores cluster and database configuration information. Specify a cluster file system file or a shared raw device containing at least 100MB of free space that is accessible from all of the nodes in the cluster.

OCR Configuration

Normal Redundancy
Choose this option to enable the Oracle Clusterware to manage OCR mirroring. You will need an additional 100 MB of disk space for the mirrored copy.

External Redundancy
Choose this option if you are using your disk management system to provide OCR redundancy.

Specify OCR Location: /data/ocr

Specify OCR Mirror Location:

Help | Installed Products... | Back | Next | Install | Cancel

ORACLE

Figure 6.14: *External Redundancy Screen*

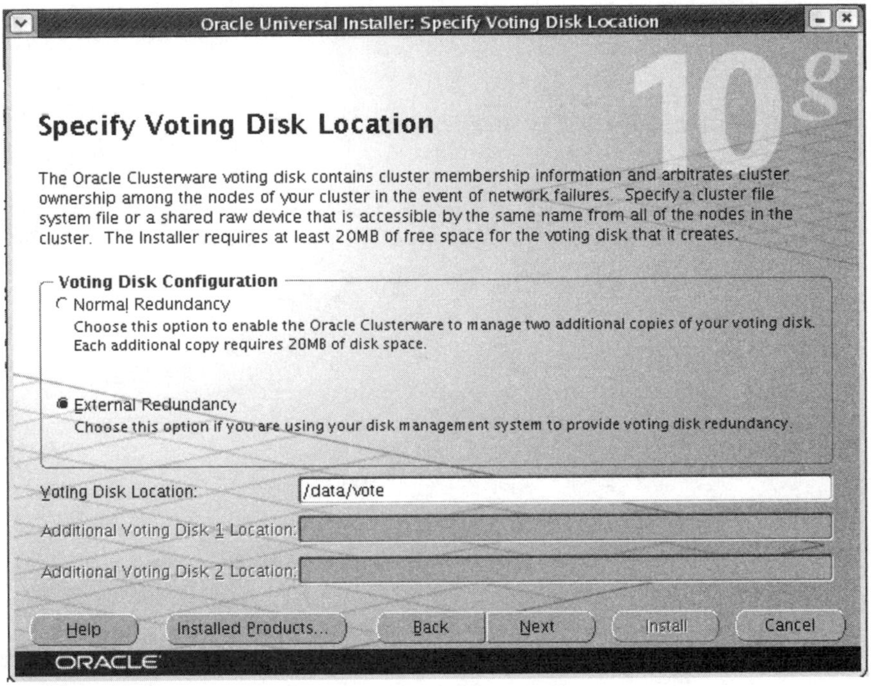

Figure 6.15: *Specifying Voting Disk Location*

Finally, the clusterware installer will ask for the nodes in the cluster in which to propagate these same settings. Since there is only one physical node in this *pseudo-RAC* setup, that is all that will be displayed, as shown in Figure 6.16. If there were other actual RAC nodes, there would merely be additional entries – one for each additional node. This completes the clusterware install process, so on to the Oracle software install.

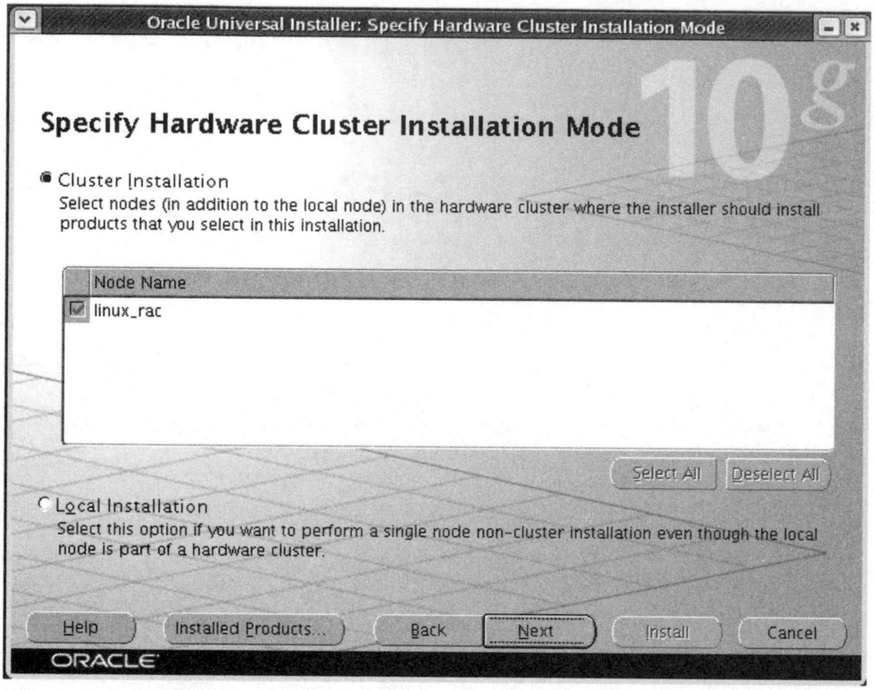

Figure 6.16: *Single Node in Pseudo-RAC Setup*

The database install is performed as before by choosing all the same options as was done in the previous chapter. To accomplish this task, export ORACLE_HOME = /home/oracle/product/10.2.0/db, and then run the database's installer via the *runInstaller* script. With the database install process, database creation is the next step. It is good to note that this might be the right place in which to shutdown the VMware image and make a backup copy. That way it will be easy to get back to this point easily if it becomes necessary to refresh the virtual machine to a prior pristine state.

Create the RAC Database

Unlike the prior chapter, for this *pseudo-RAC* setup, Oracle's Database Configuration Assistant (DBCA) will need to be run twice. The first time will create a single RAC instance on a single Linux node. Then the second time, DBCA will be asked to create a second instance on that same node. And voila! There is now more than one instance operating against a single database. The only real difference is that these two instances are not on separate Linux nodes, but rather the same node. This may be considered cheating a bit, but for non-production and non-testing use, this setup requires the minimum resources to deploy.

There should be a very distinct difference noticed immediately when running DBCA in a cluster enabled environment. The very first screen should prompt for which type of database: Real Application Cluster (RAC) databases or single instance databases, as shown in Figure 6.17. If it does not, then once again backtrack and verify the prior steps were done properly. Of course, it is best to choose the first alternative – RAC.

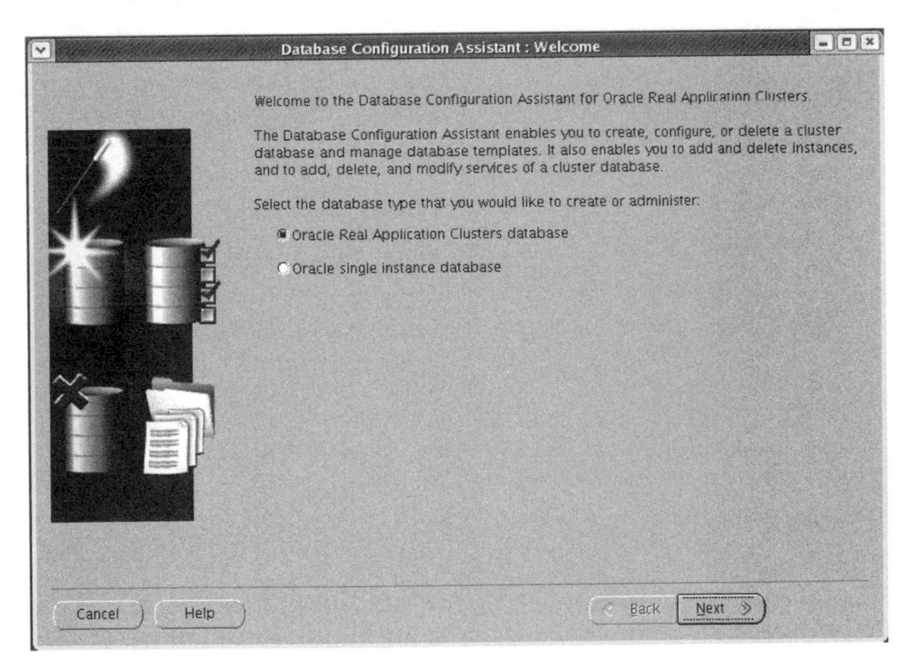

Figure 6.17: *Choosing RAC Database*

In step 1 of the DBCA wizard, choose to create a database. A RAC node selection screen should be displayed as shown in Figure 6.18. Very similar to what was done in the prior section for the clusterware installer's hardware selection, indicate to DBCA which nodes will participate in this RAC cluster database and, hence, which nodes DBCA will need to run scripts on to actually create that database and any node specific portions, i.e. redo logs, rollback segments and such. As before, since there will only be the one node, that will be the only option. This will result in a single instance being created on a single node, which may not seem too useful. But do not worry – that second node will be added shortly.

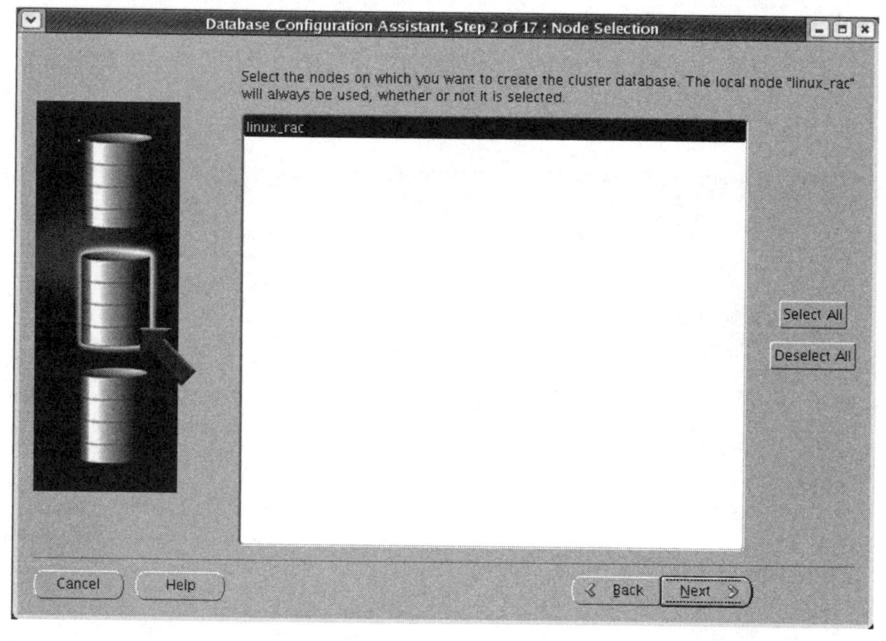

Figure 6.18: *Node Selection Screen*

Next, DBCA will prompt for the "Global Database Name" and "SID Prefix." In this example, "RAC" was indicated for each. At this point, DBCA will realize that it needs to create virtual IP addresses to support creating the database with this name. The dialog box shown in Figure 6.19 will appear. It indicates that the Oracle Virtual IP Configuration Assistant (VIPCA) needs to be run. But note that while the dialog indicates it is located under the database or "db" Oracle Home, it is actually under the cluster ware or "crs" Oracle Home. So the following two commands need to be issued instead as root:

- export ORACLE_HOME=/home/oracle/product/10.2.0/crs
- $ORACLE_HOME/bin/vipca

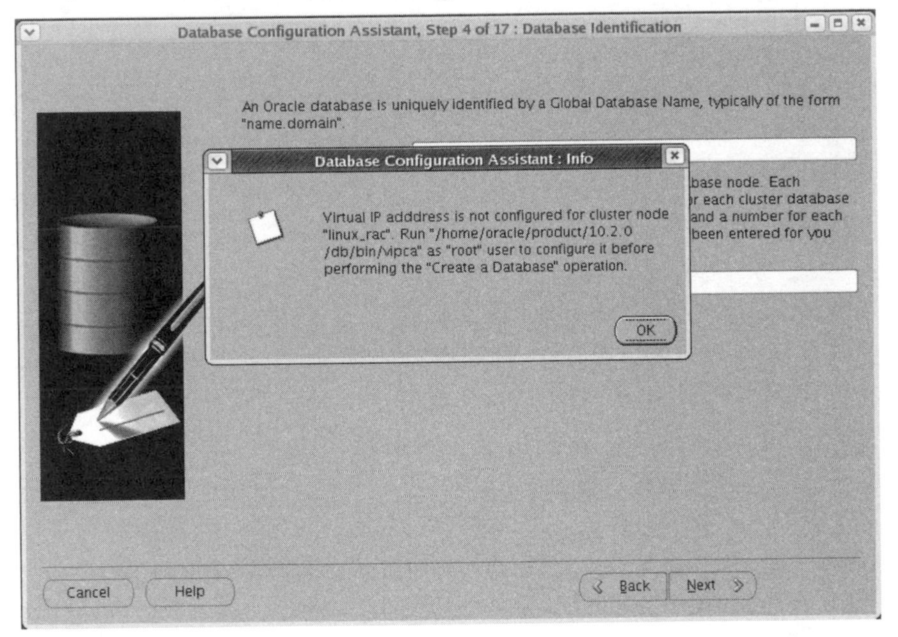

Figure 6.19: *Screen with Dialog about VIPCA*

VIPCA should then recognize the Oracle public network adapter, i.e. eth0, as the one to which to add the virtual IP address. Once again, the virtual IP address mechanism is required for both load balancing and fault tolerance reasons. In effect, Oracle will be creating some network loopback adapters and the necessary trickery or redirection to make the RAC database instances totally accessible via that new virtual IP address. That is why the one IP address is needed in the hosts file for *linux_rac-vip*. In step one of the VIPCA wizard, "eth0" will be identified as the correct "public" network adapter. Then in step 2 the *linux_rac-vip* alias and IP address will be provided as shown in Figure 6.20.

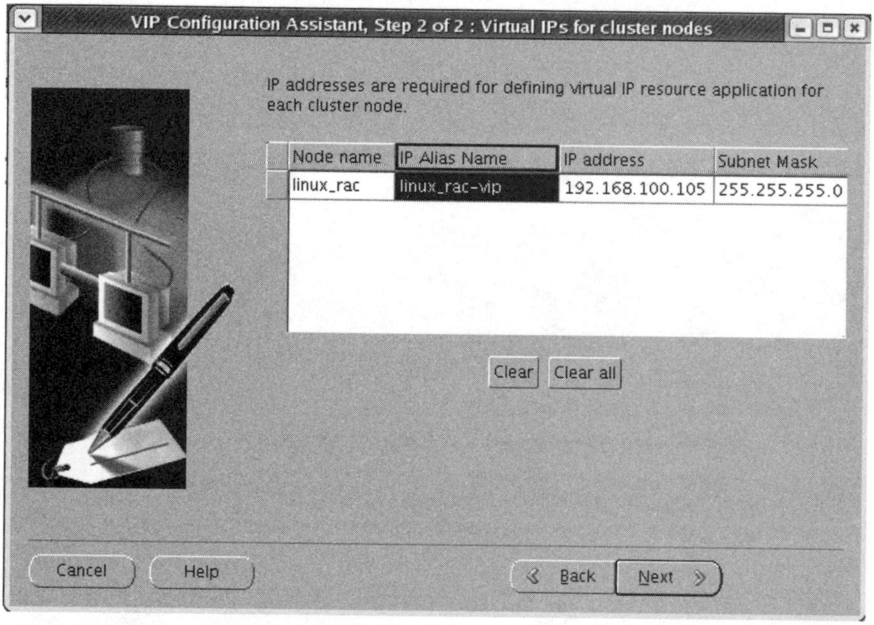

Figure 6.20: *Providing Alias and IP Address in VIPCA*

VIPCA will then go off and create everything necessary to support this network setup. Now it is time to return to some of the more typical database creation questions, such as how and where to store the database files.

Step 7 of the database creation wizard will offer a RAC database three choices as shown in Figure 6.21, all of which are "shared" disk resources, meaning more than one node can concurrently access those files as block I/O devices without locking or blocking issues. In this case, choose "Cluster File System" since you Oracle's ocfs2 is being used.

Special Note: The "Raw Devices" choice only applies when raw devices are truly being allocated directly to Oracle for data files. If some of the other options are preferable, such as the earlier mentioned choice to use Linux loop back devices to create raw devices to then allocate to ASM to manage as if real disks, then choose ASM. However, if a host raw device is mapped to a virtual machine disk, then the raw devices choice would apply.

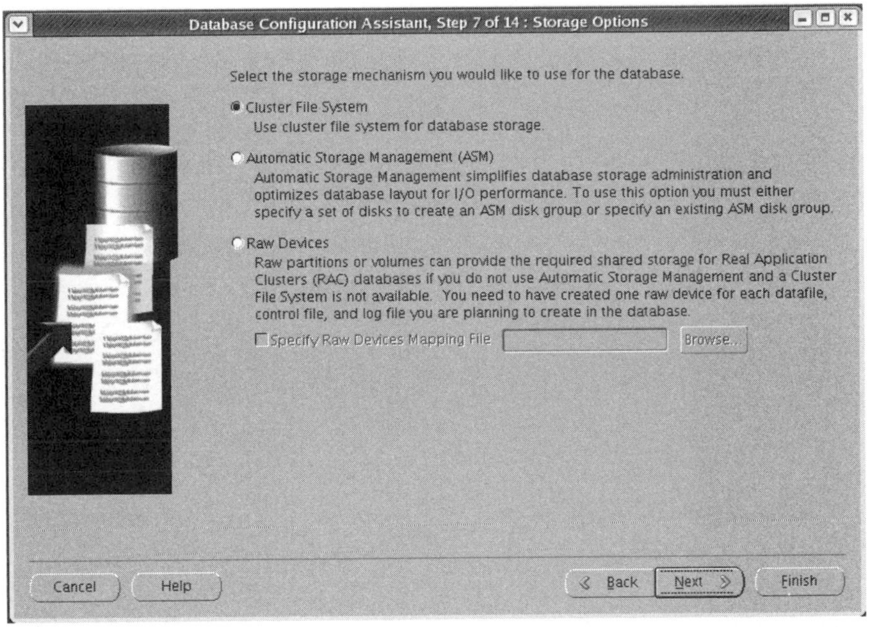

Figure 6.21: *RAC Database Choices*

Then, on step 8 of the database creation wizard as shown in Figure 6.22, simply choose "Use Common Location for All Database files." That centralized location will be located on the ocfs2 mount point: /data. DBCA will thus create all the control files, redo log files, and data files under this location. In addition, note that the OCR and voting disk were here as well under /data since these files must be concurrently accessible also.

Special Note: Do not try to cheat and use one of the standard Linux file systems such as ext2 or ext3, because the DBCA may appear to successfully create the database – or not. But even if it does so, problems will be encountered later on while Oracle has multiple instances trying to access the same files at the same times. In that case, the RAC cluster may hang or corrupt its files. So please make 100% sure to be using a clustered file system or Oracle's ASM.

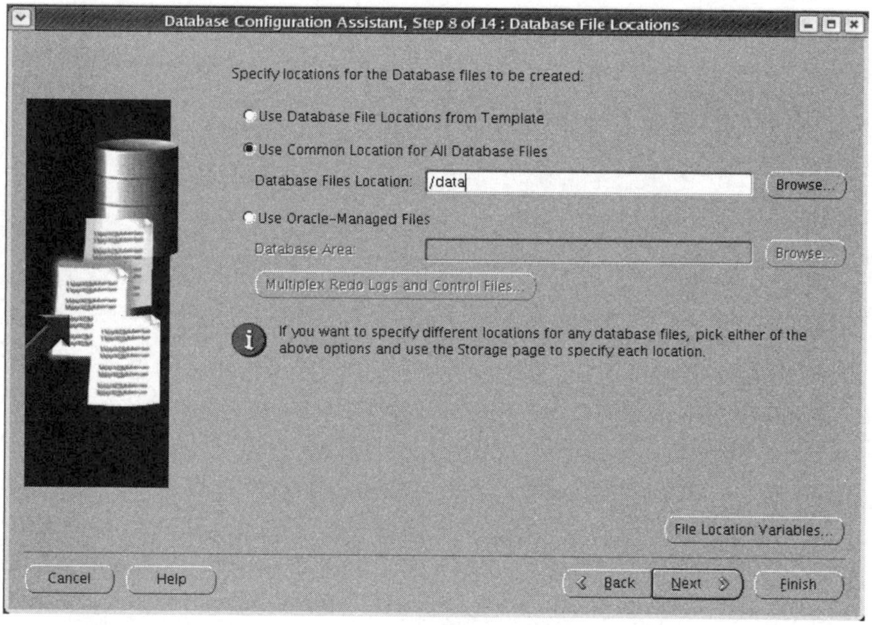

Figure 6.22: *Database File Location Screen*

Finally on step 9 of the database creation wizard, there will be a prompt for the service name for the database. Do not attempt to name it the same as the global database name or SID prefix. So in this example as shown in Figure 6.23, the service is named RACDB for the RAC global database name. Just remember what name is used since this will be the one name for which the listener process will be listening for and the service name that will be referenced in other SQL Net configuration files, such as both the host and external client tnsnames files. Note that the TAF Policy options refer to this RAC database's Transparent Application Failover setting. It defaults to none, but it is probably more realistic to set it to basic. However, remember that this is just a single operating system node. So in reality, nothing is to be gained with this setting other than appearing closer to a real world scenario.

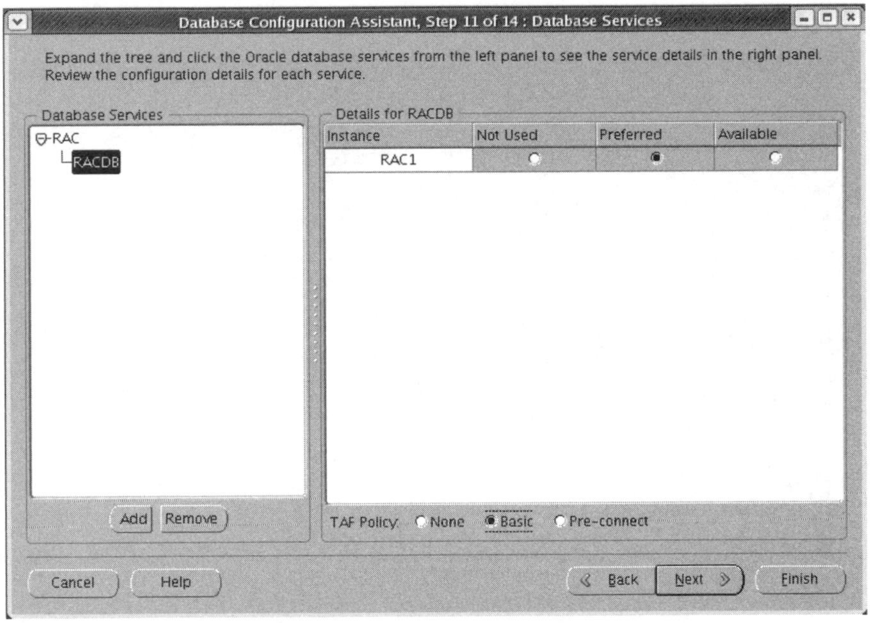

Figure 6.23: *Creating Database Service Name*

DBCA will then create a single RAC database instance on the one Linux operating system node. Now it is time to add that second instance.

First, run DBCA a second time and again choose to work with *Real Application Clusters databases*, choose *Instance Management* as shown in Figure 6.24, and then choose *Add an Instance*. DBCA will display a cluster selection screen once again, just like the two times covered before and also shown in Figure 6.25. Then choose the one and only RAC database available. For this example, this choice is RAC. DBCA will offer the default SID name for that new instance, which can be overridden, and it will create that second database instance on the one and only node. There will now be a two instance RAC cluster running on a single Linux node. If everything is properly configured, then DBCA will not take long to perform this operation. Remember, to add an instance just means to create the node specific items – not to run the entire database creation process. So do not be too surprised if this process takes just a few seconds to run.

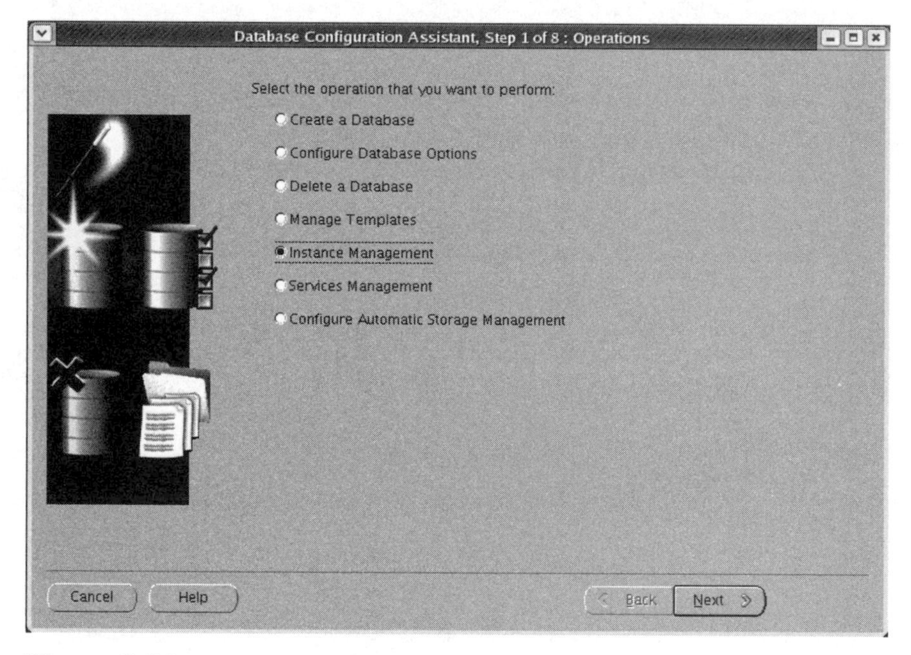

Figure 6.24: *Instant Management Screen*

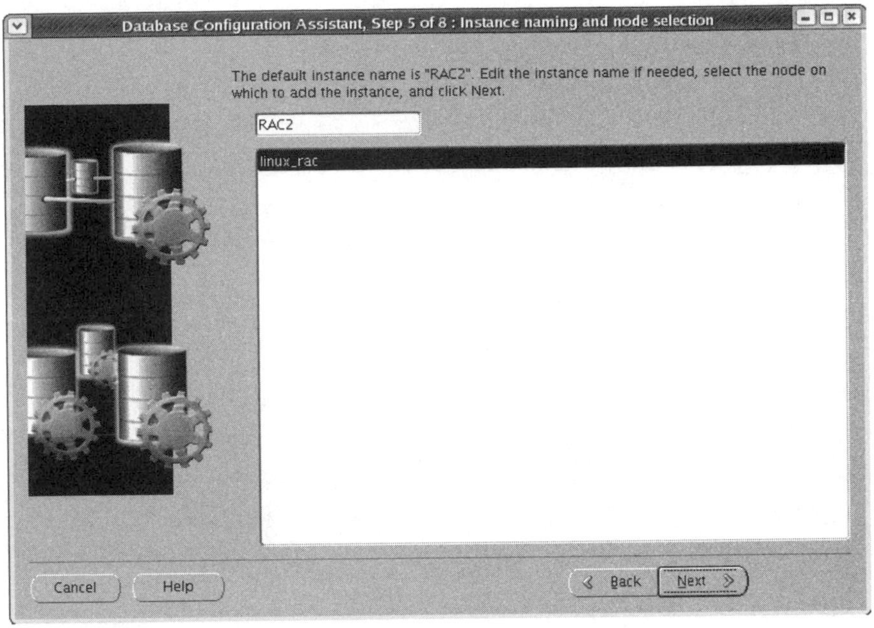

Figure 6.25: *Creating an Instance*

RAC Auto-Start

All that is left to do is to configure the Linux node to autostart the Oracle RAC cluster. That requires just three easy steps.

1. Create auto start script /etc/init.d directory/dbstart_auto.sh

```
ORACLE_HOME=/home/oracle/product/10.2.0/db
export ORACLE_HOME
su - oracle -c "$ORACLE_HOME/bin/srvctl start nodeapps -n
linux_rac" > /dev/null
su - oracle -c "$ORACLE_HOME/bin/srvctl start database -d RAC" >
/dev/null
```

2. Create auto stop script /etc/init.d directory/dbshut_auto.sh

```
ORACLE_HOME=/home/oracle/product/10.2.0/db
export ORACLE_HOME
su - oracle -c "$ORACLE_HOME/bin/srvctl stop database -d RAC" >
/dev/null
su - oracle -c "$ORACLE_HOME/bin/srvctl stop nodeapps -n
linux_rac" > /dev/null
```

3. Then execute the following commands to set it all up

```
ln -sf  /etc/init.d/dbshut_auto.sh   /etc/rc0.d/K10dbshut
ln -sf  /etc/init.d/dbshut_auto.sh   /etc/rc6.d/K10dbshut
ln -sf  /etc/init.d/dbstart_auto.sh  /etc/rc2.d/S99dbstart
ln -sf  /etc/init.d/dbstart_auto.sh  /etc/rc5.d/S99dbstart
```

Conclusion

In this chapter, the last chapter's example was expanded upon to build more than a simple single instance database –a *pseudo-RAC* cluster was built. The idea was again to provide a simple yet effective demo and/or experimentation playground for working with RAC on a machine with limited capacity while requiring the least amount of physical resources. While this is not truly a RAC cluster and not really supported by Oracle it looks and acts real enough for its intended limited purposes. In fact, this setup will run quite well on a reasonable laptop/notebook by today's standard like one with a dual core processor, 2 GB of memory and at least a 60GB disk drive. This author has been successful going to four RAC instances under such a setup on a notebook with 4GB of memory with no real loss of performance.

The next chapter will examine creating true RAC deployments in the virtualization world and how the capabilities are expanding in this realm.

True RAC Setup

CHAPTER

Wiring together virtualized RAC servers requires lots of cable, patience and valium!

Overview

Up until now, the virtualization of Oracle databases has been examined in two key modes: single instance deployments and *pseudo-RAC* deployments on a single virtual node. But with the obvious future slant of companies moving more aggressively towards utilizing RAC to leverage lower cost hardware, some attention needs to be given to doing true RAC in the virtual world as well. That leads to the first decision of whether RAC and virtualization even belong together in the same sentence.

RAC and VM Compatibility

Some people are of the opinion that Oracle RAC and grid architecture are exclusive of virtualization. In fact, many of those people would go so far as to argue that database servers in general should not ever be virtualized. The thought is that database servers are so specialized, high demand (especially for I/O) and mission critical that they are not reasonable candidates for virtualization. That might have been true a year or two ago when virtualization was still relatively new and the hardware had not branched so pervasively into multi-core CPUs with tons of cheap memory. But times have changed and so have the limitations, if they ever actually existed at all.

Most database servers these days are overkill in terms of CPU capacity versus their average needs and often more than their peak needs as well. So, as has always been true, I/O is the limiting factor of gravest concern when dealing with databases. Even with today's powerful SAN, NAS and iSCSI disk subsystems, I/O still remains the greatest limiting factor in most cases. The higher bandwidth and capacity still exist on the CPU and memory side of the equation. That is why the average database server has extra and, therefore, underutilized capacity.

What has happened is that the fundamental grid concept has been fully realized through virtualization. It is really feasible to treat servers, even database servers, as nothing more than resources that can be allocated and load balanced as necessary. It is no longer necessary to build stand-alone islands of server functionality, so all of the computing resources can be better utilized. This process actually lowers the total hardware costs to boot. Plus, this provides a "greener" solution as well, which is highly desirable these days. It is truly a win-win scenario from many different angles and worth doing.

Here is a diagram in Figure 7.1 that just a few years ago might not have seemed reasonable, but with which the industry has become more comfortable today. Look closely at what this picture describes – mixing database platforms and database instances across a virtualized I/O subsystem. This actually has been done for quite some time and people do not think too much about such configurations anymore other than generally agreeing that gone are the days of walking into a server room and pointing to a particular database's disks. So now assume, for sake of argument, there is general agreement on this picture. Note that while the I/O workload is mixed with SQL Server and Oracle on same disks; the database platforms are physically separated across physical servers.

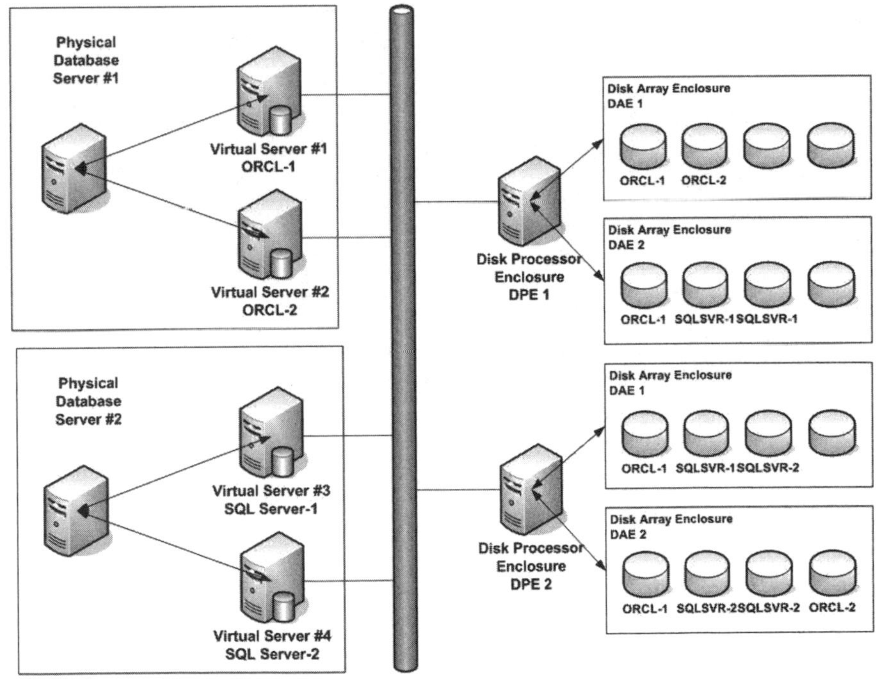

Figure 7.1: *Mixing Database Platforms and Instances – 1 Side*

So what happens if the following very minor changes are made to the diagram as shown in Figure 7.2 and now allow mixing the database platforms on the left hand side as well? Some people might argue that this is the first step onto a very slippery slope. This author simply believes that this next level of abstraction and virtualization has already been generally accepted and it is possible to both effectively and efficiently mix database platforms and database instances across hardware on both sides of the equation. So please look closely at this picture, because the water is going to be "muddied up" a wee bit more.

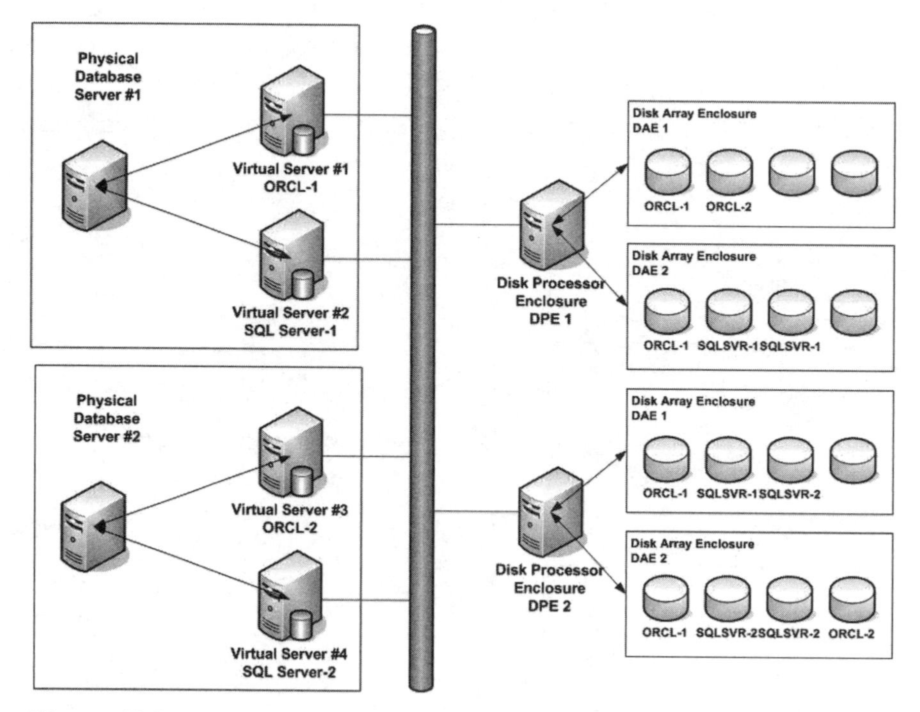

Figure 7.2: *Mixing Database Platforms and Instances on Both Sides*

The next logical step along this virtualization progression might well be something along the lines of the diagram in Figure 7.3. At first glance this picture may seem odd: why would anyone host multiple RAC nodes on the same physical servers like this? But do not jump too quickly to any conclusions. If the primary worry is load balancing, then what is really wrong with this concept? Consider a desktop computer that has a quad core CPU with 8

GB memory – that can be built for about $500. Many of today's servers come with dual quad core CPUs and at least 8 GB of memory with eight core and greater CPUs already being designed for next year and beyond. This growth of the gap between CPU vs. I/O bandwidth really shows no indication of slowing anytime soon. So this picture becomes a reasonable reality in the very near future, if it is not already. One should not arbitrarily try to stand in the way of hardware evolutions or revolutions occurring around us. Embrace the picture below as being both reasonable and likely to occur sometime soon.

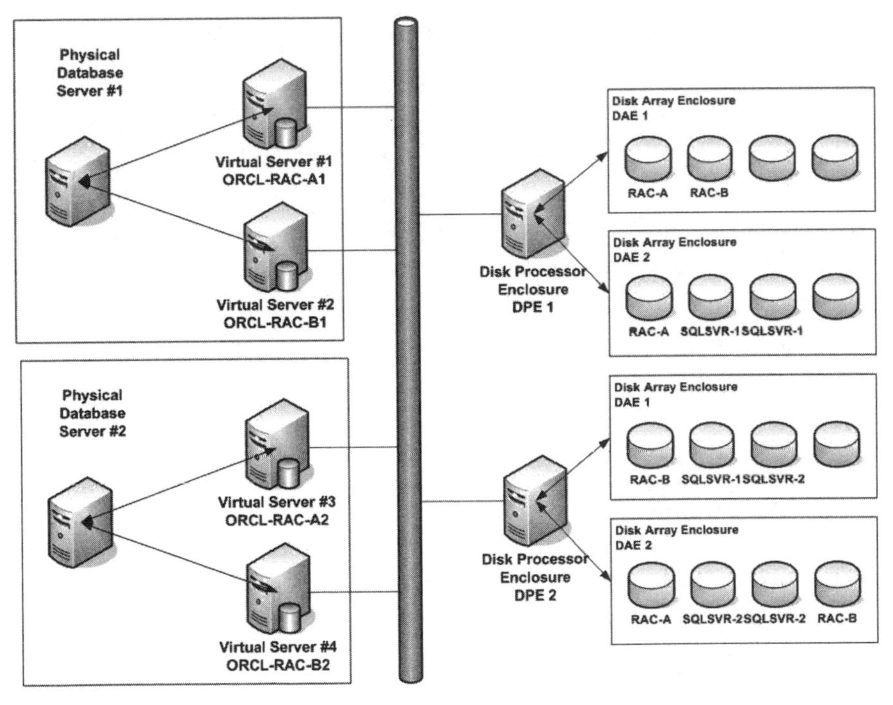

Figure 7.3: *The Evolution of hardware*

Thus, RAC and virtualization are indeed compatible and make sense in many and ever growing scenarios. From here, this chapter will explore how one would construct such a setup. As with the prior chapter, the instructions will be kept to a minimum under the assumption that the reader has read the prior two chapters and fully understood all the steps therein explained. The reader is free to return to those chapters as during this chapter.

Preparation

There are two key differences to address during the configuration of the virtual host machines for a true RAC setup. First, there will be multiple virtual hosts that require both a coherent and coordinated setup with the usual minimal installation goal at heart. And second, that this is the first configuration "recipe" where it is for much more than just simple demonstration purposes. One would likely only incur such added premium costs and additional setup complexities for a real-world test or production database. Therefore, one needs to more carefully plan and define the underlying or foundational architecture so as to maximize both its effectiveness and efficiency. It should come as no surprise that this genuine or real world database virtualization project requires something more than freeware.

As such, it is strongly recommend that any virtualized database environment be built using VMware's ESX Server product line – using their true enterprise scalable, "bare metal" hypervisor solution. Reviewing the comparison from chapter 2 shown in Figure 7.4, ESX essentially provides a pre-canned mini-OS/hypervisor combination that has been streamlined and optimized for large scale virtual deployments. Moreover, VMware ESX provides several features that examine what a virtualized Oracle RAC database requires and for which there may well be no other or easier solution. Plus, it removes one extra layer of overhead, i.e. the host operating system, from the technology stack.

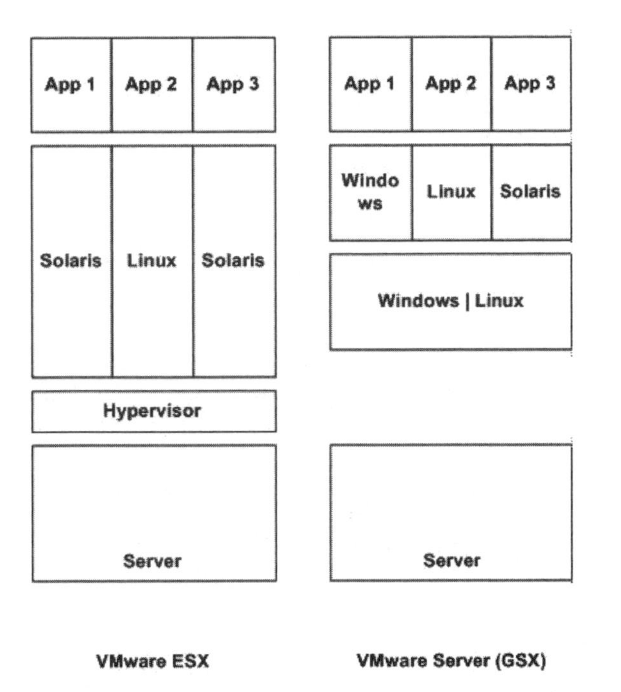

Figure 7.4: *Paravirtualization and Full Virtualization*

There are many other advantages to VMware ESX Server over the free GSX Server. ESX Server is more scalable in terms of CPU and memory and also runs faster, which permits more virtual machines per host. Furthermore, ESX Server offers versions that support many extended enterprise requirements such as VMware's VMFS cluster file system, high availability, disaster recovery, and backup/recovery.

As with any complex technical undertaking, another primary critical success factor is access to the proper knowledge. Many DBAs will often purchase books to support their project needs. So an Oracle Linux DBA might buy some Oracle DBA books, a Linux reference and possibly a book on tuning Oracle for Linux. There would be nothing special about this practice. So it should come as no surprise that it is strongly recommended to add a couple of VMware books to that wish list. The following are two books that this author has found invaluable:

- VMware ESX Server: Advanced Technical Design Guide [ISBN 0-9711510-6-7], an invaluable reference text for all things related to VMware Server configuration & tuning
- Rob's Guide to Using VMware, 2nd Ed [ISBN 90-808934-3-9], a concise and informative "best practices" and general advice book

Finally, be prepared to apply many new techniques in the virtualized world and do not be afraid to make a few educational mistakes along the way!

Special Note: As with the prior chapter, this focus during this chapter will be on those items of major significance from the prior two chapters, as they relate to configuration and setup.

VMware Host Settings

While the ESX Server host setup may offer some additional challenges that will not be covered here, the two issues of paramount importance relate to the host's network setup. Looking at the RAC overview diagram in Figure 7.6, there needs to be at least two, if not three, distinct network segments. So how are the RAC cluster's public, private and storage network segments separated? Also, how does one bridge or bind multiple network cards together to increase overall bandwidth? There has really been nothing seen so far in the free VMware Server to accommodate these needs and this is why one must upgrade to VMware ESX Server for success.

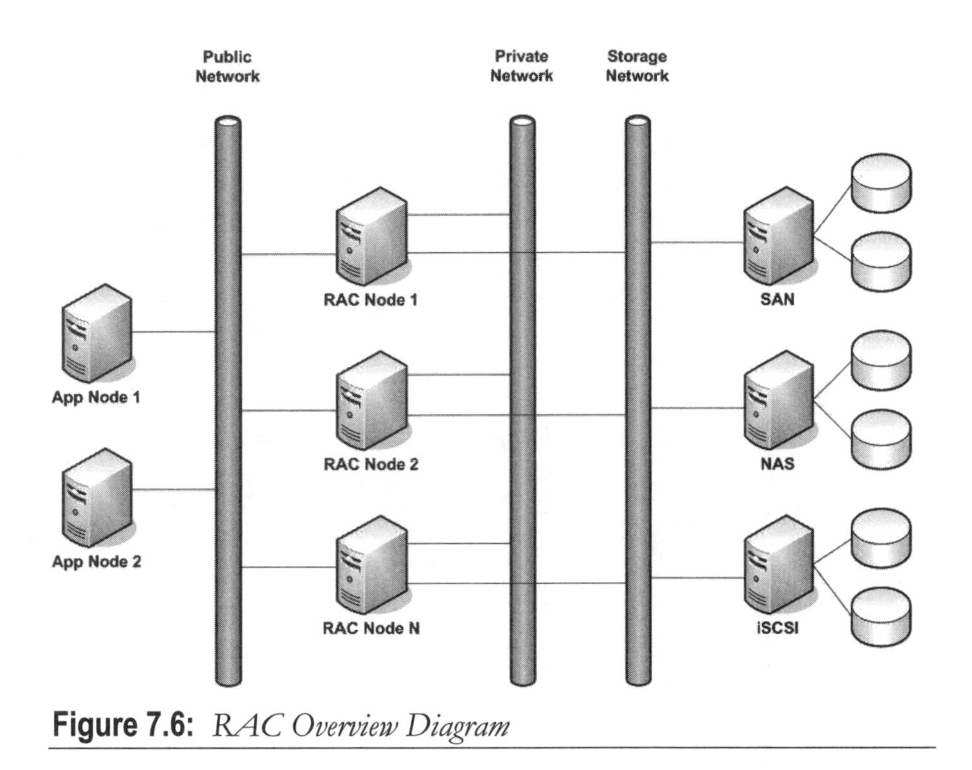

Figure 7.6: *RAC Overview Diagram*

VMware Server ESX offers a feature called *virtual switches* to address the network segment separation issue. Network segments can either be separated using VLAN segmentation (as with physical switches) or by simply defining dedicated virtual switches for each different network segment's need. VMware ESX Server also possesses a feature called *NIC Teaming* that combines physical network adapters to support the virtual switches. It is very much like what Linux refers to as bonding and Windows as bridging.

The next step is to examine how just one physical database server has to be configured to host two individual instances from two different RAC clusters (Figure 7.7). Assume that there will be three network cards per RAC database instance - one for the public network and two teamed ones for the private network - since interconnect traffic and latencies are critical to RAC performance. Thus, just counting the network entities alone on this one physical server, sixteen different items would have to be configured at the hypervisor level. Throw in the client operating system network adapters, there would now be some twenty network items per node. So for a ten node RAC cluster, there would be 200 network items to configure! Take a look back at the cartoon at the very start of this chapter and it should make a heck of a lot more sense now!

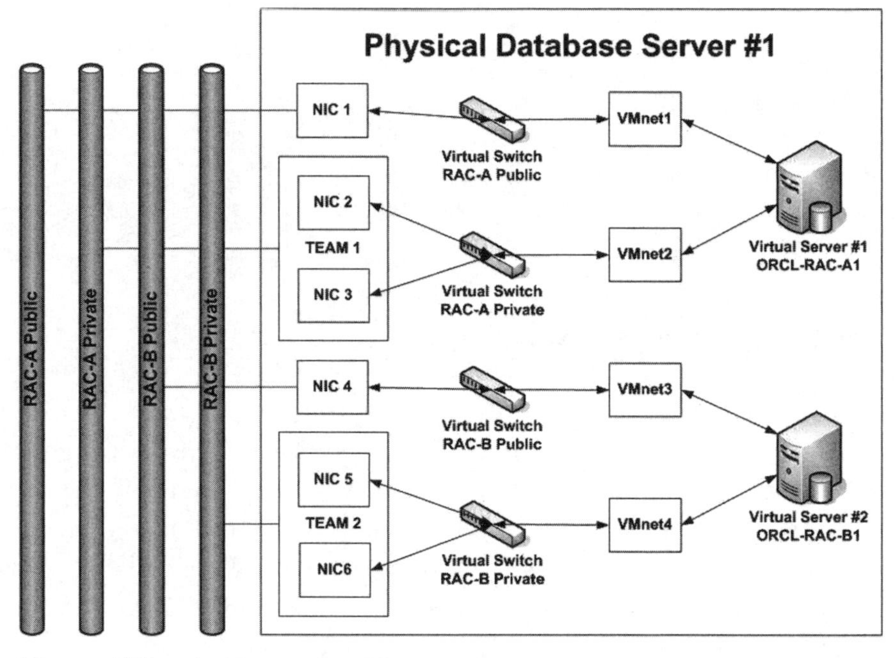

Figure 7.7: *An Example of Hosting Scenario*

Virtual Machine Setup

There is but one recommendation for this level of the configuration. It would be most efficient to allocate database I/O activity disks, spindles or LUNs (logical units) as "physical disks" – think of it as raw devices. Then use Oracle ASM to allocate, manage and control all such devices. There is no reason to add the extra level of overhead because ASM is a perfect solution for virtualization and worth recommending whether one is doing RAC or just single instance databases. In fact, at the Oracle 11g training, an Oracle instructor said that some 60+% of new RAC cluster deployments were choosing ASM, and that even 25% of all general purpose, non-RAC deployments were as well. Because VMware Server ESX is so stripped down, one can also appreciate the free Logical Volume Manager (LVM) and file system capabilities that ASM makes available to a virtualized RAC database – and all for no additional cost.

Remaining Steps Same

From here on in the setup process is pretty much the same. Since the lower levels of the configuration have been abstracted, the steps up to this point have covered all the bases. Now the process is like any other multi-RAC node install and configuration process. It will be necessary to verify that each node's hardware, bios, firmware, operating system or hypervisor, device drivers and optimizations are identical or as close as possible if there are fundamental hardware differences across the RAC nodes. Either SSH (Secure Shell) or RSH (Remote Shell) will also need to be configured so that both the Oracle Universal Installer and Database Configuration Assistant can function for all the nodes.

Other Things that Matter

When asked if other things matter, of course the answer can always be yes. That is just the nature of the beast in the Oracle world. But are there any items that specifically warrant being pointed out? Here are a few of the more urgent ones.

First, be careful not to create more than one virtual machine on a specific physical server that services the same RAC database.

While there is actually nothing fundamentally wrong with this (refer back to our *pseudo-RAC* chapter), this should only occur in limited scenarios where it is specifically dictated. For example, one way to dynamically manage or allocate excess capacity for better load balancing might be to create additional RAC nodes across whatever resources are currently available – even if that means creating more than one RAC instance on the same physical server. However, it might be wiser to simply allocate additional dynamic resources (e.g. CPU, RAM, priority and such) directly to the RAC instance nodes as necessary. There is software on some virtualization platforms to manage this and, in some cases, to even automate it.

Second, take some additional time to think about the computing center's network cabling and switch setup. Remember the 200 network items that would need to be defined in the twenty node RAC cluster? It may seem advisable for the physical switches to use VLAN to route segments of traffic. It may also be necessary to plan for more Ethernet segments given the increased complexity and additional moving parts such a virtualization strategy causes. The point is that the network and its wiring may be much more involved and more closely concentrated than is generally customary. Who knows – it might be that virtualization is the last straw which "breaks the camel's back," and finally requires upgrading to ten gigabit Ethernet.

For no matter what the joke may be about it – size really does matter. It is not uncommon to leverage lower cost components in the virtualized information center. But be very careful not to accidentally create any artificial bottlenecks by sizing hardware without properly accounting for the highly concurrent nature and utilization of all the virtualized resources. Very few have enough practical experience yet in hardware sizing for such heavy usage, so error on the side of caution when in doubt because the entire virtual infrastructure can only be as strong as its weakest link.

Hence, there are now many major, hidden interdependencies between the systems. Look again at this picture from earlier this chapter. We have two physical servers each hosting one half of two RAC clusters. This particular solution is more about freedom to allocate resources rather than fault tolerance, so it is a legitimate scenario that you may well encounter. Look again at Figure 7.3 and think about the interconnect traffic and the desire to keep it humming along. That alone will be the example's "Achilles' heel".

If one tries to reduce the now 400 network item count (200 network items per physical server, and two physical servers) and attempts to use fewer network cards or share the private network segment, both databases might be slowed down. Furthermore, sporadic and thus irreproducible performance issues might be introduced where one database or its nodes cause side effects on the other RAC database. The fundamental point is virtualization means "shared everything" – and that necessarily means more dependencies outside the normal project scope. In fact, it is not uncommon to relocate entire databases in the virtual world once such performance issues arise. But that is actually the key strategic benefit of this approach: resources can be allocated, wherever, and whenever they are needed. That increases resource utilization, reduces excess capacity, lowers total hardware costs and even yields greener information centers.

The only other key area that is significantly different is the monitoring, diagnostic and tuning efforts, but that will be addressed in the next two chapters. Just remember that in the virtualized world, there are many more moving parts, and thus, more to watch and/or tweak.

Conclusion

This chapter explored the real world applicability of virtualized databases – specifically, for Oracle RAC. The conclusion was that virtualization and RAC are compatible. Furthermore, that this technology progression is really nothing more than finally realizing the promise of "grid." The key areas to concentrate upon were the lower levels of the virtualization technology stack, and expressly to rely upon VMware Server ESX for production use for both performance and scalability reasons. Moreover, acknowledge that the configuration of key virtual resources at this level is critical, especially when trying to limit any unplanned consequences from interdependencies. Finally, that the front and rear end processes, such as planning and monitoring, require additional effort. But not to worry, because in the true virtualized world where everything is just a resource, things can be moved as needed. So the flexibility inherent within virtualization can sometimes be the single most valuable reward and worth the price of admission all by itself.

Performance Comparisons

"Yes, I was an NCAA all star for 5 years".

Overview

What do politicians, statisticians, pollsters, benchmarks (even industry standard database benchmarks) and the cartoon above all have in common? Namely, that they can be easily manipulated to tell one what one wants to hear. That does not mean that they do not have value. Nor does it mean they should be skipped or totally ignored. It just means that each needs to be weighed within their appropriate context and with some level of overall skepticism as to general applicability. The same is equally true of this chapter's material.

This chapter is not going to present facts and figures to convince anyone to follow any particular course of action or setup configuration. It is merely going to present enough material so that readers can see and deduce that virtualization alternatives are both reasonable and manageable. Yes, all the benchmarks within this chapter could have run faster without the additional overhead virtualization necessarily introduces. But then all the other many benefits that have been examined thus far would not be realized, especially not the increased flexibility, which often is enough justification by itself for many people given today's cheap yet powerful hardware. So the goal here is to provide convincing evidence that virtualization is a viable alternative for database infrastructure possibilities. Then it is up to the reader to verify whether it actually is a good fit or not for any particular project needs.

The Benchmarking Process

The science of benchmarking is sometimes better practiced as an art. What the means is that simply and/or blindly running industry standard benchmarks like the TPC-C, which mimics OLTP (online transaction processing) workloads, might be reasonably expected to yield conclusive results. But there are so many variable factors in the hardware and software configurations that people often obtain unexpected, non-repeatable or just plain wrong results. That has, in turn, led to much skepticism regarding the science.

When doing database benchmarks on simple non-RAC and non-virtualized databases, it is wise to allocate double the time one thinks it will take to run the benchmark in order to properly configure and tune all the components that contribute to the overall performance result. So if it will take a week to run the tests, allocate three weeks to complete the entire project. That usually loses most people's attention or buy in – which is too bad, because most benchmarking projects fail simply due to improper planning for time.

The second greatest contributor to significant benchmarking problems is confining one's scope of the project to just the database. Contrary to some DBAs who subscribe to the Galilean logic that the world revolves around their Oracle databases, that is not the way to successfully benchmark. If people doing benchmarking do not fully understand and optimize every contributing portion of the entire technology stack, then the results are relatively worthless. Far too many benchmarking projects deemed a failure where the team had no idea how their disk LUNs were allocated, what stripe depth and width they were using, how many physical spindles their database had access to, and many other key critical success factors. Yet they fully expected to arrive at meaningful results.

Virtualization by its very nature adds another level of abstraction, and therefore, more moving parts. Complete and intimate knowledge of the entire technology stack is even more of a must in this complex scenario. So the next two sections are going to address some benchmarking "quick bites," best practices, and recommendations. For a more thorough review of benchmarking, the following book is recommended: *Database Benchmarking: Practical methods for Oracle & SQL Server* [ISBN 0-9776715-3-4].

Benchmarking Quick Bites

Benchmarking is not a subject worthy of major contemplation, yet many people ascribe too much effort in over-thinking about various minutia aspects of the science. Many benchmarking projects have people worrying far too long about ancillary questions like the five issues stated below. They are just not worth diverting attention from the main issue at hand, which in this book will be examining database performance on a virtualized platform. So they are stated here to get them totally out of the way so there is no need to be concerned about them anymore.

1. Which Operating System yields better benchmark results – Windows or Linux?

   This is the most controversial and difficult issue. This author freely admits to being a UNIX and Linux bigot, but that is because he has been doing UNIX twice as long and likes the scripting languages. Yet Windows has matured so much in the past few years as a server platform that this question seems fair game and on everyone's minds. Figure 8.1 shows the results of the TPC-C benchmark performed on identical hardware using both 32-bit and 64-bit versions of Windows 2003 Server Release 2 and CentOS 4 Update 3 (a free Redhat enterprise variant).

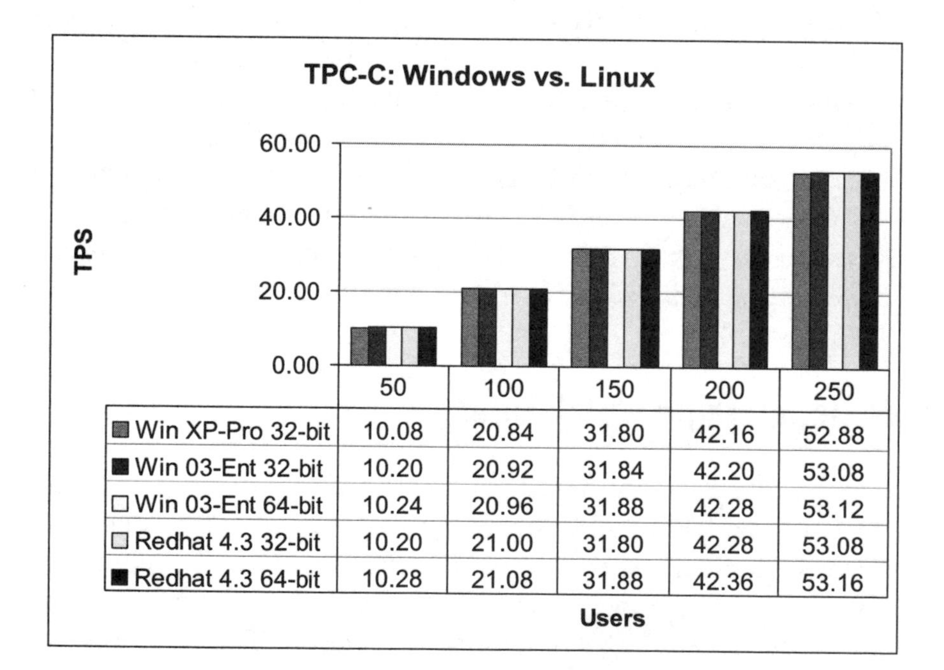

	50	100	150	200	250
Win XP-Pro 32-bit	10.08	20.84	31.80	42.16	52.88
Win 03-Ent 32-bit	10.20	20.92	31.84	42.20	53.08
Win 03-Ent 64-bit	10.24	20.96	31.88	42.28	53.12
Redhat 4.3 32-bit	10.20	21.00	31.80	42.28	53.08
Redhat 4.3 64-bit	10.28	21.08	31.88	42.36	53.16

Figure 8.1: *Comparison Chart of TPC-C Benchmark*

Looks like a dead heat. So whichever operating system the DBA is more comfortable with or already has more system administrators for – that is the most logical choice.

2. How many bits are best - 32 or 64 – and can that effect the operating system choice?

   64-bit UNIX servers have been around for many years. But 64-bit Windows has only just become a reality. While Windows NT ran on the DEC Alpha, it never really became mainstream. This author has been partial to AMD's Athlon-64 and Opteron processors; that is, until mid 2006, when Intel's 2nd generation dual core CPUs came out and performed so amazingly. So now it is just a matter of whichever hardware's current price gives the most bang for the buck with energy consumption and room cooling being included secondarily in the TCO calculations. But do 64-bits really make a noticeable difference? According to the chart in Figure 8.1, it does not. That is because 64-bit's primary advantage is increased addressable memory. In Figure 8.2 are the results of the TPC-C benchmark performed once again, but now with increasing amounts of total system and database allocated memory.

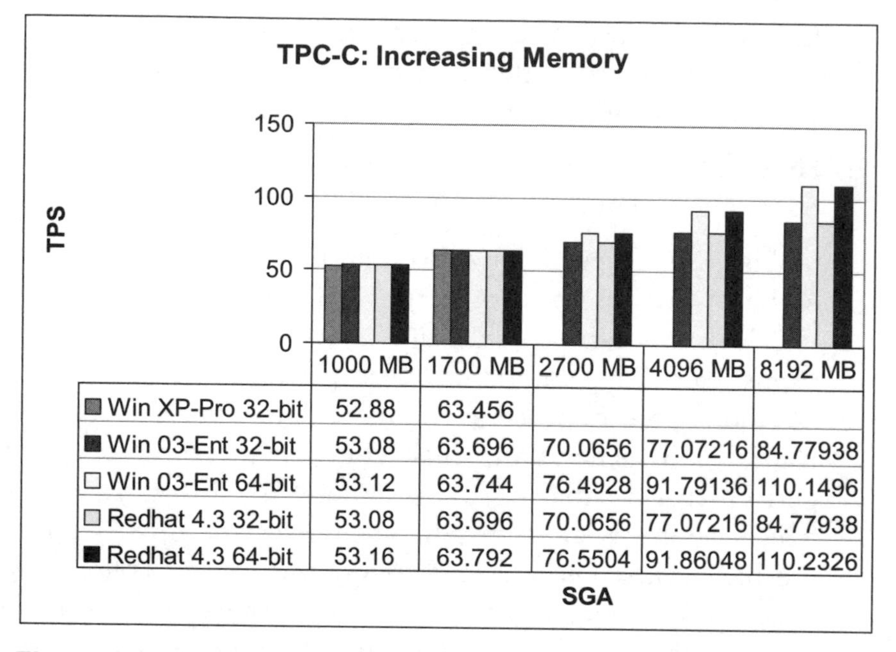

	1000 MB	1700 MB	2700 MB	4096 MB	8192 MB
Win XP-Pro 32-bit	52.88	63.456			
Win 03-Ent 32-bit	53.08	63.696	70.0656	77.07216	84.77938
Win 03-Ent 64-bit	53.12	63.744	76.4928	91.79136	110.1496
Redhat 4.3 32-bit	53.08	63.696	70.0656	77.07216	84.77938
Redhat 4.3 64-bit	53.16	63.792	76.5504	91.86048	110.2326

Figure 8.2: *TPC-C Comparison Chart with Increasing Memory*

Once again, there are some very clear results. If the server has 2 GB or less, then there is really no discernable difference. But as the server's memory increases beyond 2 GB, now the 64-bit advantage comes into play. Even though some databases like Oracle have 32-bit linkage options to "trick-up" the database into accessing slightly more memory (known as the large memory model), they only increase it up to a certain point. It is clear the extra memory for both system and database makes ever increasing performance improvements a genuine reality. So for anything over 4 GB, it is a no-brainer – go with 64-bits. However, there is one caveat: sometimes 32-bit Linux works better with certain hardware such as drivers and iSCSI, and newer database options (e.g. ASM, OCFS, etc).

3. Which database benchmarks best – Oracle 10g, SQL Server 2005 or MySQL 5.0?

Here goes another very controversial question, which is limited to just the three databases that come up most often – skipping DB2-UDB, PostgreSQL, or any other database is not an intentional slight. Once again, this author proclaims Oracle prejudices right up front as he has been working with Oracle for 22+ years. It is also worth mentioning that database vendors generally frown upon posting benchmarks, especially comparative ones. But nonetheless, this one question gets asked all the time. Thus, in Figure 8.3 are the results of the TPC-C benchmark performed once again, but now for just those three databases asked about most often.

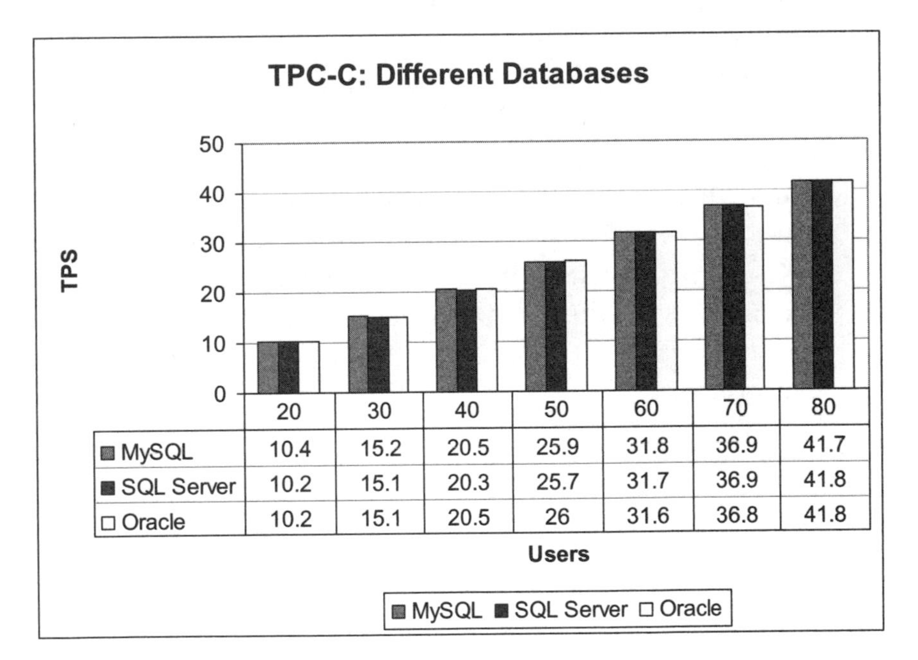

Users	20	30	40	50	60	70	80
MySQL	10.4	15.2	20.5	25.9	31.8	36.9	41.7
SQL Server	10.2	15.1	20.3	25.7	31.7	36.9	41.8
Oracle	10.2	15.1	20.5	26	31.6	36.8	41.8

Figure 8.3: *Comparison Chart of Three Databases for Benchmarking*

The performance results are again a dead heat. Consequently, whichever database is most comfortable or for which there are already database administrators – that is the logical choice. Of course, there are also the cost differences amongst the vendors, but since no one ever pays list price, it is hard to give accurate TPC-C ratings that include those subjectively variable costs. So by sticking just to the technologies themselves and their relative benchmark performance, there is yet again another tie!

4. How does one determine the maximum concurrent OLTP users a server can sustain?

   This is always a tough question to answer because people usually want to hear something like a Dell 1850 can handle N concurrent users. But even servers in the same family and with the same amount of memory can vary by number of CPUs, CPU clock speed, CPU cores, and cache sizes. So it is not easy to compare servers unless nearly identically configured boxes are compared. Plus, identical network and disk I/O scenarios need to be compared. Assuming that has been done, then the question is how to read the benchmark results to accurately decide what the maximum concurrent user load is for that server. Figure 8.4 shows the results of the TPC-C benchmark performed yet once again, but now for just one server where the inflection point we determined, i.e. the point where the user load begins to negatively affect the response time.

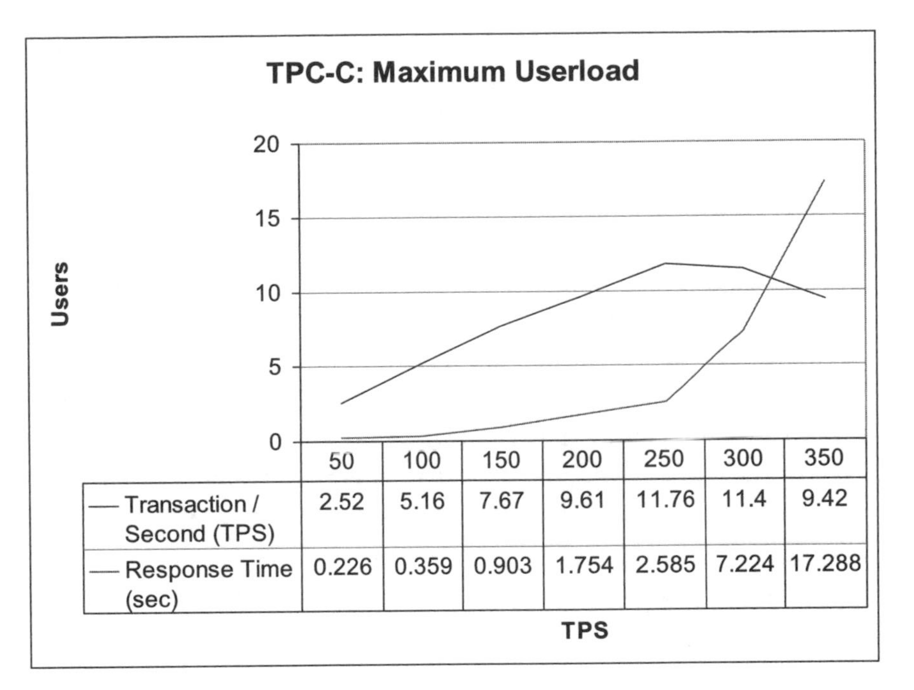

	50	100	150	200	250	300	350
— Transaction / Second (TPS)	2.52	5.16	7.67	9.61	11.76	11.4	9.42
— Response Time (sec)	0.226	0.359	0.903	1.754	2.585	7.224	17.288

Figure 8.4: *TPC-C Benchmark Single Server Chart*

If end-users require less than a two second response time (which seems to be the number often quoted), then 200 concurrent users is the likely stopping point. But the server in this example could support as many as 250 concurrent users before the response time reaches the point of unacceptably steep increase. Note that in this particular case, that is also about the same point where the TPS rate begins to flatten or decrease. It is not always this obvious because sometimes the two inflection points do not line up so perfectly. But when in doubt, always go with the response time for TPC-C or OLTP type transactions.

5. How does one determine the maximum size data warehouse a server can sustain?

   This is always a tough question to answer because people most often want to hear something like how many Dell 1850s are needed for N terabytes. As before, even servers in the same family and with the same amount of memory can vary by number of CPUs, CPU clock speed, CPU cores, and cache sizes. So, once again, it is not easy to compare servers unless nearly identically configured boxes are compared. Plus, one also needs to compare identical network and disk I/O scenarios, especially the disk I/O, because the TPC-H results are governed most by the number of spindles. But again assuming that is done, the question is how to read the results to accurately decide what the maximum sized data warehouse is for that server or servers. Figure 8.5 shows the test results of the TPC-H benchmark for several increasingly powerful Oracle RAC server configurations accessing 300 GB spread across multiple SANs and over 100 disks (with many, many thanks to Dell and their Linux testing lab for making these results possible).

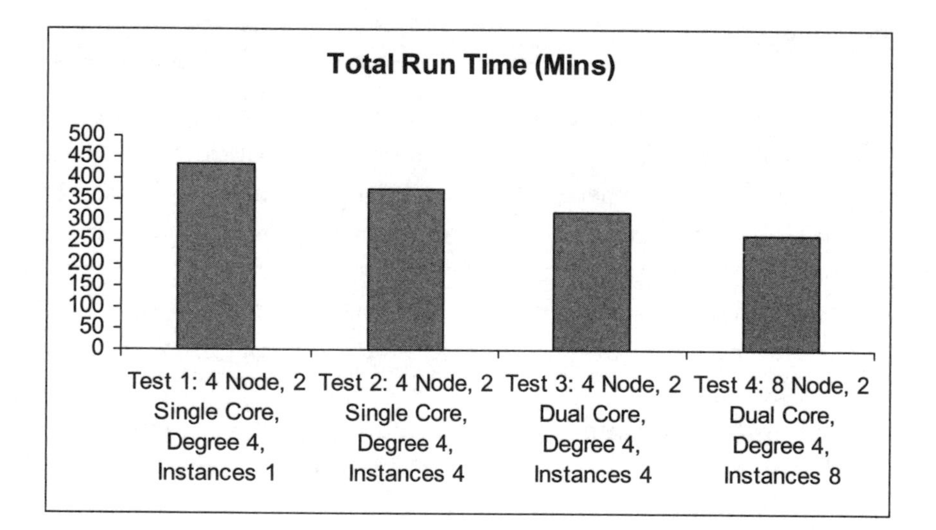

Figure 8.5: *TPC-H Benchmark Server Configurations – Total Run Time*

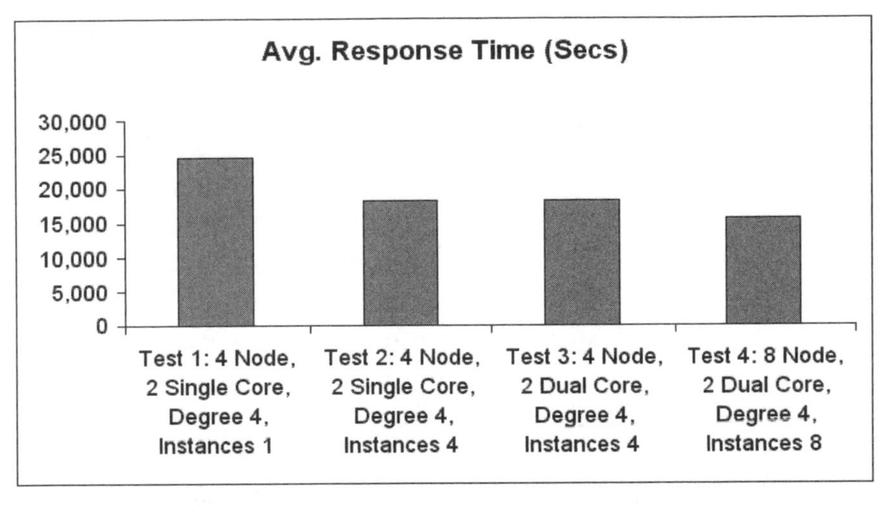

Figure 8.6: *Benchmark Server Configurations – Avg. Response Time*

Look at both the total run time and average response time for the TPC-H, which should be in step with each other. Do not be dissuaded by the large time values – the TPC-H queries are very complex and often take hours or even days apiece for large data warehouses. In Figure 8.6, the best hardware setup takes about five hours to run with an average response time of approximately four hours. However, the actual 22 queries' response time results are highly skewed by just a few that take a majority of the time to run. So if users can accept potentially four-hour run times for highly complex decision support queries, that 8 node cluster would suffice. If not, instead of adding more nodes, purchase more spindles since it is not uncommon for terabyte sized warehouses to have 500-1000 spindles for optimal results.

Benchmarking Best Practices

Sometimes the easiest way to get people to more closely adhere to recommendations or best practices is simply tell them the things not to do. It is often easier to do great work when there is a shorter list of what not to do. So here are the top ten mistakes often seen in the benchmarking world – avoid them!

1. A benchmarking tool like Quest's Benchmark Factory is being used, so that is all that is needed.

   Wrong. It is highly recommend that anyone doing benchmarking read the specifications for whatever industry standard tests they are going to perform. Software to automate these tests will ask questions or present options that cannot really be defined unless their context is understood and that is defined in the specs.

   For example, the highly popular OLTP test known as the "TPC-C Benchmark" defines scale factor as follows (http://tpc.org/tpcc/spec/tpcc_current.pdf):

Section 4.2.1: The WAREHOUSE table is used as the base unit of scaling. The cardinality of all other tables (except for ITEM) is a function of the number of configured warehouses (i.e., cardinality of the WAREHOUSE table). This number, in turn, determines the load applied to the system under test which results in a reported throughput (see Clause 5.4).

Section 4.2.2: For each active warehouse in the database, the SUT must accept requests for transactions from a population of 10 terminals.

   So when a tool like Benchmark Factory asks for the scale factor, it does not mean the number of concurrent users, but rather the number of warehouses. Hence, a scaling factor of 300 means 300 warehouses and, therefore, up to 3000 concurrent users.

   This requirement to read the spec is critical as it will be an underlying issue for every remaining misconception and problem that will be covered in the next few pages.

2. The system has an expensive SAN, NAS or iSCSI disk array, so there is no need to worry about configuring anything special for I/O.

   Incorrect. The size, type and nature of the test may require radically different hardware settings, even all the way down to the deepest level of the SAN. For example, a data warehousing test like the TPC-H is best handled by a SAN who's "read-ahead" and "data-cache" settings are set more for read than write, while the OLTP TPC-C would benefit from just the opposite. Relying on defaults can be a really big mistake.

   Likewise, the SAN hardware settings for stripe depth and stripe width should be set differently for these different usages. Plus, the file system and database I/O sizes should be a multiple of the stripe depth. In fact, a common rule of thumb is:

```
Stripe Depth >= db_block_size X db_file_multiblock_read_count
```

   Furthermore, selecting the optimal hardware RAID (Redundant Array of Independent Disks) level quite often should factor in the benchmark nature as well. Where OLTP might choose RAID-5, data warehousing might be better served by RAID-0+1.

   Finally, the number of disks can also be critical. For example, TPC-H tests start at around 300 GB in size. So anything less than 100 spindles at that size is generally a waste of time. As one scales larger, 800 or more drives becomes common as the minimum recommended setup. The point is that no SAN cache is ever large enough for monstrous data warehousing queries' workload.

Up to 500% result differences has been seen when varying SAN settings and number of disks.

3. The default operating system configuration can be used right out of the box.

   No. Most databases require some prerequisite operating system tweaks and most benchmarks can benefit from a few additional adjustments. For example, from 50-150% benchmark differences have been seen running TPC-C benchmarks for both Oracle and SQL Server by adjusting but one simple file system parameter. Yet that parameter is not part of either database's install or configuration recommendations.

   Now one might argue that this step can be skipped since it will be an "apples to apples" comparison because the machine setup will be the same across tests. True, but why potentially wait three times as long for worse results? Since a 300 GB TPC-H test can take days just to load, efficiency is often critical in order to meet your time deadlines.

4. The default database setup/configuration can be used right out of the box.

   Wrong. While some databases like SQL Server might be universally useful as configured out of the box, other databases like Oracle are not. For example, the default number of concurrent sessions for Oracle is 50. So if one tries to run a TPC-C test with more than 50 users, there is already trouble ahead.

   Likewise, the nature of the benchmark once again dictates how numerous database configuration parameters should be set. A TPC-C test on Oracle would benefit from *init.ora* parameter settings of:

```
CURSOR_SPACE_FOR_TIME = TRUE
```

```
CURSOR_SHARING = SIMILAR
OPTIMIZER_INDEX_CACHING = 80
OPTIMIZER_INDEX_COST_ADJ = 20
DB_FILE_MULTIBLOCK_READ_COUNT = 2
```

As much as 533% performance improvement has been witnessed from adjusting these five parameters alone (see test runs #2 - #4 in Figure 8.7), so imagine what a careful review of all the database configuration parameters for the test nature could provide!

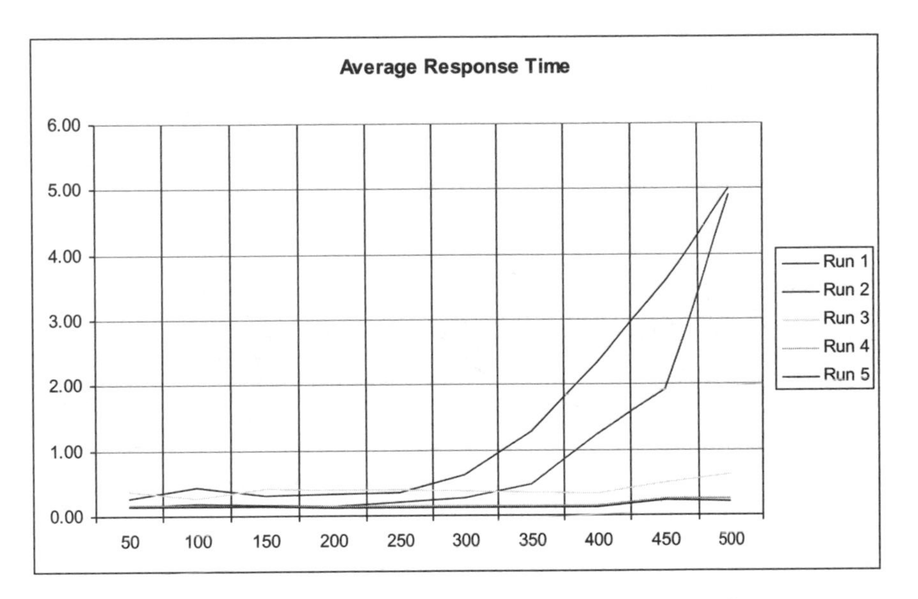

Figure 8.7: *Chart with Adjusted Database Configuration Parameters*

5. Tools like Benchmark Factory will create optimally designed database objects such as tables, indexes and partitions for hardware and database setup.

   Off the mark. Software like Benchmark Factory is simply a tool to automate the complex and tedious process necessary to execute a benchmark. For example, the TPC-H is a collection of 22 very long and complex SELECT statements against a very simple database design with some really big tables. It tests the database optimizer's efficiency in handling complex statement explain plans and their executions.

While one can let tools like Benchmark Factory default object sizing and placement, it is unadvisable to do so. When presented with the scaling screen shown in Figure 8.8, where the benchmark scale and resulting database object size are selected, it is highly desirable to manually instruct Benchmark Factory about how to size and where to place those database objects via the "Advanced Creation Option" button.

This launches a screen where tablespace, partitioning, sizing, and other selections specific to setup can be specified. This can easily result in orders of magnitude performance differences, so it is almost always worth doing.

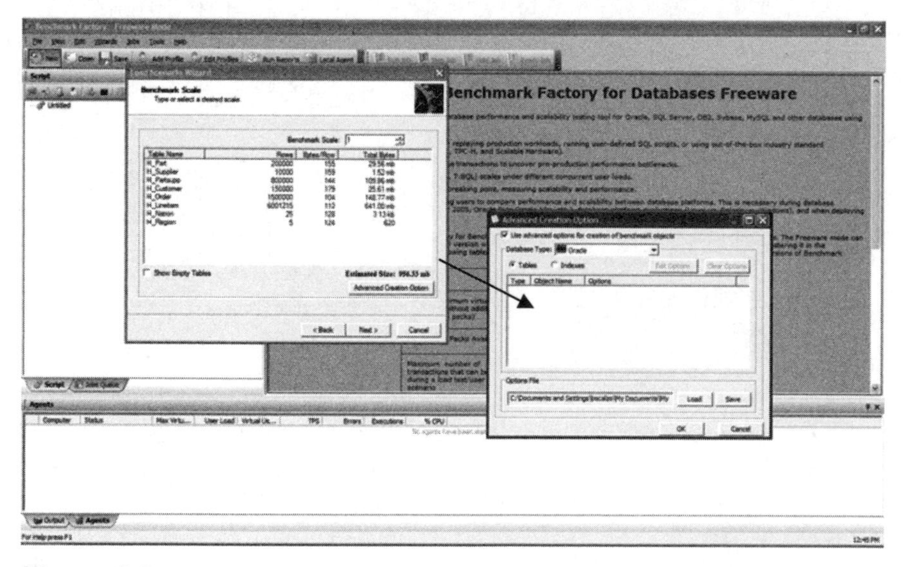

Figure 8.8: *Benchmark Scaling Screen*

6. Tools like Benchmark Factory will automatically monitor, tune and optimize all hardware, operating system and database configuration parameters.

Incorrect. As stated before, software like Benchmark Factory is simply a tool to automate the complex and tedious process necessary to execute a benchmark. Appropriate tools like Quest Software's Spotlight for Oracle, Performance Analysis, and Toad with DBA Module are needed to monitor, diagnose or tune/optimize the database for such tests. Remember, benchmarking tools are simply load generators.

7. A DBA is not needed to perform benchmark tests – anyone technical can do it.

   Wrong. Look at all the issues above again because sometimes database developers or other technical database-savvy people may not be cognizant or authorized to make such decisions. The key point, once again, is that benchmarking requires more than just someone to run tests; it requires someone who knows benchmarking and can speak to all the issues. Otherwise, the results will not really reflect what the hardware could do. Also, 500+% performance differences are more than just background noise – a strategic decision could be made with such misinformation.

8. Database vendors can very easily be compared on the same hardware platform.

   Possibly. If there are DBAs who can address all the above issues for each different database platform, then by all means, yes. Otherwise, the databases cannot be reliably compared by merely installing and running the same test for each. There are far too many dependencies and variables to trust such a simplistic approach.

9. Transactions per Second (TPS) are what matter most in benchmarking.

   Rarely. TPS is one of the most misleading values, but everyone seems to focus on that one first. Here is an explanation. As the number of users or tasks being performed increases, by definition the TPS increases. At some point it may plateau, but what does that indicate? Look at the chart below in Figure 8.9:

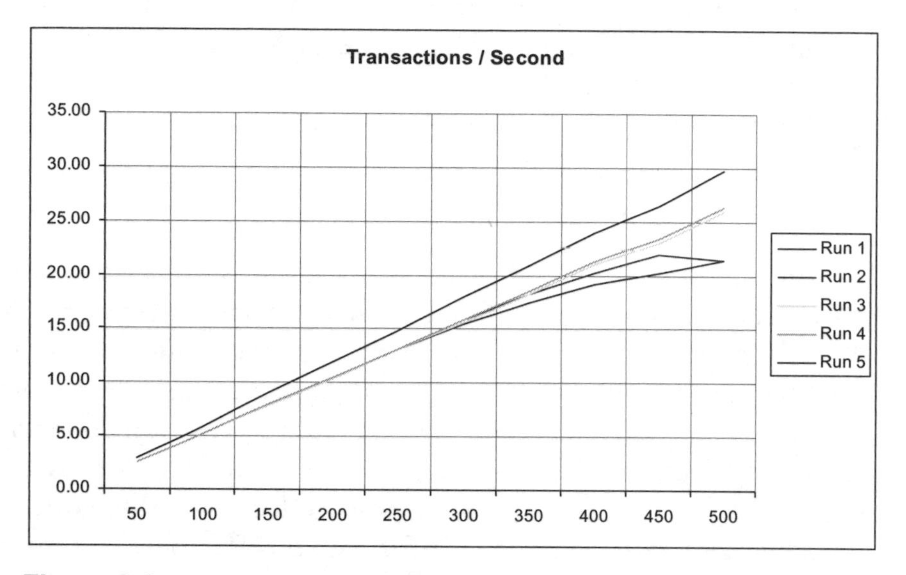

Figure 8.9: *TPS Chart – Per # of Users*

This is the TPS results for the exact same test runs shown by the graph in Figure 8.7 where there was a 533% improvement in the average response time. Not only does that mean something real in user or SLA terms, but it is obvious and understandable. The way the TPS chart really should be examined is via the first derivative of the various lines for that is where to look for the best growth in slope. Above, that is obviously the line for test #5. But where does one quit? The chart in Figure 8.7 is more useful because if the user says they require response times <= 2 seconds, then simply look for where the line crosses that boundary and that is the maximum.

So if the default database setup had been used, the server would run out of gas slightly over 300 concurrent users. But the final tweaking efforts seem to indicate an actual result of almost double that number!

10. It will only take a few days to benchmark everything.

    Never. Almost universally, the proper setup of all the dependent components can take a week or two and when doing large scale benchmarks, can sometimes add up to a week for data loads and index creation. So make sure to carefully project enough time to complete such efforts because there will be surprises along the way, even if the advice give above is not followed. For more info, again see the benchmarking book: *Database Benchmarking: Practical methods for Oracle & SQL Server* [ISBN 0-9776715-3-4].

Selecting Among Benchmarks

The necessary first step to effective and useful benchmarking is to decide what specifically to test. Now this is a very subjective exercise that can be answered differently by different people, or even differently by the same people at different times. There really is no single, definitive benchmark to run under all circumstances – it all depends. Nonetheless, here are some useful guidelines:

- For OLTP database workloads, consider industry standard TPC-C or newer TPC-E
- For Data Warehouse workloads, consider industry standard TPC-H (requires many disks)
- For narrow/specific application workloads, replay associated Oracle trace files
- For broad/overall application workloads, replay transactions using Oracle 11g's new Real Application Testing (RAT)

However, do not feel compelled to strictly adhere to the original benchmarking specification or guidelines entirely, as there will obviously be mitigating or special circumstances in many real world scenarios.

One question that quite often arises when discussing benchmarking on virtualized machines is, what about using VMware's new VMark benchmark? The problem with this benchmark is that it is far too broad or generic and therefore, not database nor Oracle specific. By testing along all of these six categories - email server, java server, standby server, web server, database server and file server - the benchmark is really meant to test the relative efficiency of the underlying virtualization architecture and specific platforms' execution. Thus, this book will stick with using the simple TPC-C OLTP test which is quite familiar to many DBAs.

Relative Results

So far there has been quite a substantial build-up to what is actually a very short and concise set of benchmark observations as shown in Figure 8.11. The same hardware was tested under four different configurations and the TPC-C benchmark was run for 50 to 500 users, watching that the response time remained two seconds or less.

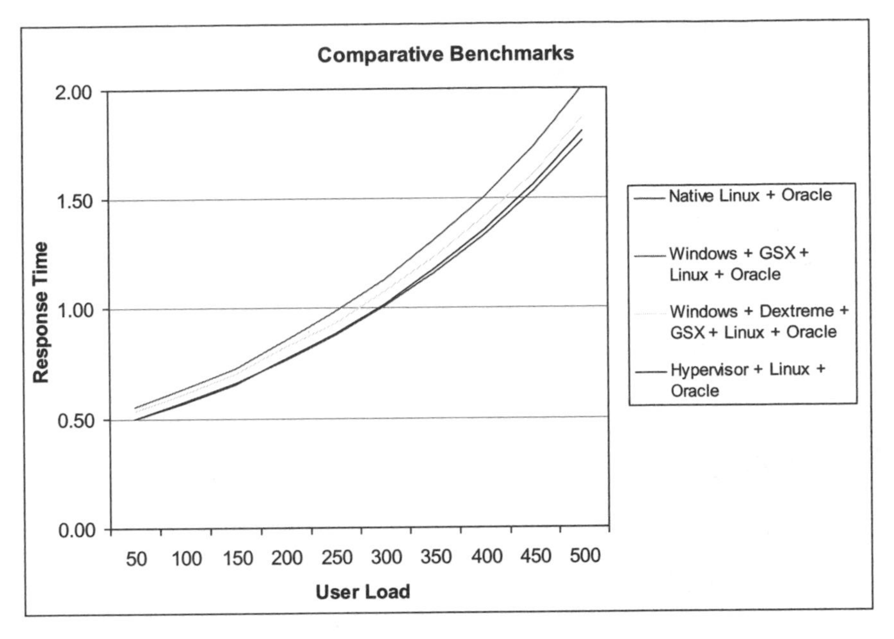

Figure 8.11: *Comparison Chart of Various Benchmark Configurations*

Remember, the goal was to show that virtualization is a reasonable choice. Furthermore, that the various virtualization options offer different performance characteristics, one of which should suffice for specific database needs. So the results will now be examined and the findings summarized.

Of course, the native operating system serves as the baseline. Two clear observations surface immediately and both of which make sense. First, the native operating system wins since it has the least amount of overhead. Second, the hypervisor based solution is very close to that of the native operating system, i.e. the hypervisor really does add very low overhead. Another finding, although a little harder to see, is that the DExtreme I/O accelerator for VMware GSX improves with increasing user load. That makes sense since it basically serves as a much smarter I/O cache than what is on the native OS file system, and it scales much better. But the biggest finding is that virtualization of the database did not cause user requirements of two second or less response time to be exceeded and that all the configurations were pretty close, i.e. no shocking surprises nor major disappointments.

Furthermore, additional tests show that as the number of databases increases and thus, the number of virtual machines, a very similar pattern emerges. That confirms the objective: virtualization is, in fact, a reasonable alternative for database deployments.

Conclusion

The objective of this chapter was to observe the performance characteristics of a virtualized database solution to see if it made sense to use this technology. First, what and how one would perform a successful benchmark were defined, and then how one would best interpret those results. These techniques were then applied to a range of obvious alternatives: native OS vs. VMware GSX vs. VMware GSX plus a smart cache vs. VMware ESX. Regardless of what performance pattern or characteristics the results implied, the major finding was that the database could be virtualized and still accomplish the response time requirements and all within an acceptable proximity of results that is offset by the added benefit of flexibility that virtualization offers.

Additional Tuning Thoughts

CHAPTER

Poor Oracle response time has huge productivity costs.

Overview

There are a number of great books available on the topic of Oracle database optimization and tuning. 98% of their content is directly applicable to the world of virtualized Oracle environments. So it would be presumptuous to assume that in a single chapter, the content of numerous volumes of other texts can be related. However, there are certain common sense approaches to database tuning that generally yields predictable and profitable results in almost any scenario.

Because of certain negative connotations, this approach wouldn't necessarily be referred to as a methodology or paradigm. Plus, this approach may not necessarily seem considered innovative or revolutionary. This is simply a gathering together of the best portions of various other peoples' techniques into this approach to tuning with the added feature of a final piece specific to virtualized Oracle deployments.

Two Basic Approaches

There are essentially two camps among DBAs when it comes to monitoring, diagnosing and tuning a database.

The first camp consists primarily of practitioners who treat the database as the source and target of all their tuning and optimization efforts. This is a resource utilization centric focus on tuning where the center of the universe is the database and hence, that is where the bulk of the tuning efforts are applied. These DBAs generally rely on complex scripts to calculate key database level performance metrics or ratios from Oracle aggregate performance data contained in *v$* and *x$* tables. They then seek to improve those values primarily through changing database configuration parameters. They also use this technique to incidentally identify application code, such as SQL or PL/SQL that causes those database metrics to skew and then seek to correct those as well. But they are simply fixing the application issues based upon the interpretation of database level related metrics.

This first camp often embraces sophisticated graphical dashboards which simplify the database architecture and its corresponding analysis. They rely quite heavily on GUI presentation and drill-downs of the Oracle aggregate performance data contained in *v$* and *x$* tables rather than having to develop those complex scripts, and they focus on tuning by fixing the *red gauges* indicating a database resource being stressed. Tools embracing this approach include Oracle's

Enterprise Manager Diagnostics Pack, Quest's Spotlight for Oracle, BMC's Smart DBA for Oracle and Symantec's i3 for Oracle. The key difference among these tools is their GUI content, organization, navigation and drill-down capabilities.

The second camp consists primarily of practitioners who treat the application as the source and target of all their tuning and optimization efforts. This is a resource consumption centric focus on tuning where the center of the universe is the application, so that is where the bulk of the tuning efforts are applied. These DBAs rely on application and database instrumentation trace files to identify where an application is spending too much time waiting, meaning that the end user sees slower response time, which is how most SLAs are defined. They then seek to improve those values primarily through changing the application areas where delays are excessive. They also use this technique to incidentally identify improperly set database configuration parameters that cause those delays and then seek to correct those as well. But they are simply fixing the database issues based upon the interpretation of actual application performance observations.

This second camp generally embraces a technique most often known as *Method-R*, which was founded by Cary Millsap, former VP of Tuning at Oracle and CEO of Hotsos. Method-R proposes a radically different approach: do not tune database resource usage, but rather strive to shorten the overall response time for any business critical process. Thus, instead of examining the graphical display of the Oracle aggregate performance data contained in *v$* and *x$* tables, these practitioners capture and then dissect the detailed Oracle trace file data for the process in question. They then attempt to reduce the key or major wait times experienced in order to reduce the overall response time and therefore, keep users happy with very snappy systems.

The fundamental philosophical difference between these approaches is that Method-R is proven to work where dashboards fail to determine the true problem or only do so after several iterations of hit and miss diagnostics. Furthermore, some problems exposed by the detailed instrumentation data can be hidden or impossible to spot via dashboard tools. In fact, the dashboard type tools can sometimes lead DBAs to fix unimportant or non-existent problems – sometimes even exacerbating the true underlying issue – and thus, actually making performance worse.

Why Two Approaches

It often helps to understand why things are done a certain way and tuning databases is no exception. This begs the question, "Why are there just two primary approaches to database tuning?"

Here is one hypothesis. The human brain is known to consist of two distinct hemispheres, with the following characteristics for each hemisphere listed in Figure 9.1.

	Right Hemisphere	Left Hemisphere
Specialties	▪ Copying of designs ▪ Discrimination of shapes e.g. picking out a camouflaged object ▪ Understanding geometric properties ▪ Reading faces ▪ Music ▪ **Global holistic processing** ▪ **Understanding of metaphors** ▪ Expressing emotions ▪ Reading emotions	▪ Language skills ▪ Skilled movement ▪ **Analytical time sequence processing**

Figure 9.1: *Characteristics of Right and Left Hemispheres of the Brain*

Look at the three highlighted characteristics. The first group (and especially those embracing colorful GUI dashboards) is attacking their performance issues using the right hemisphere of the brain. Whereas the second group employing instrumentation analysis such as trace files are very clearly focusing on looking at what happened when. Therefore, the second group is attacking the problem using the left hemisphere of the brain. This diagram seems to explain why there are only two ways to tune databases.

Yet a Third Dimension

DBAs generally fall into one of two camps. But consider a third dimension, the 50,000 foot view. One thing humans can do better than computers is to see the forest through the trees. Some would call this capability abstract reasoning, which www.about.com defines as the ability to analyze information and solve problems on a complex, thought-based level. Computers are really nothing more than super-fast calculators. They can run millions of well defined transactions per second. People might not be that quick but they can think, so that allows them to readily solve problems computers can not.

That is the basis for the addition of a third dimension to the practice of database tuning. While the two camps defined in the prior section tend to work predominately one way or the other, the third option prefers to do both and add an additional level of tests. These extra checks fall into one or more of the following categories:

- "Low Hanging Fruit"
- Obvious yet Overlooked
- Subtle yet Highly Critical

So database optimization and tuning efforts follow a simple three-step process which is really nothing more than a combination of all these techniques since one cannot be expected to find all the answers:

1. Ask a lot of high level, dumb questions, and verify the basics
2. Perform *Method-R*-like database application trace file analysis
3. Perform a final database "health check" using diagnostic software

The following is a real-world example of applying this comprehensive optimization and tuning process with the positive results obtained and the relative cost to do so. After examining a successful implementation of this technique, the next step will be to define a generic recipe for its successful execution. Do not be too surprised by its simplicity!

Customer X had an OLTP application deployed on an Oracle 10g RAC database on Linux. The performance was substandard and they were fully contemplating returning to large SMP boxes running Solaris, which was their historic deployment platform and comfort zone. They had unsuccessfully initially deployed the RAC Linux solution, and even paid post-deployment database tuning experts (of the right brain hemispherical nature using scripts and dashboards) to try to improve the situation. As Method-R predicts, the results were unimpressive. While the tuning experts could run reports to show that the ratios and metrics had improved by impressive percentages, the response time was actually no better. Since the cost to go backwards was deemed far too expensive in terms of reputation, they received a quote for experts who would employ Method-R software and techniques with the promise that payment would only be based upon achieving results. This was attractive to them since they had already been burned once.

However, even that reasonable estimate and its promise meant that the overall budget, including the failed tuning efforts, was going to far exceed the initial planned savings. So they were stuck between a rock and a hard spot – either go backward and suffer the loss of end user faith, or spend the second round of tuning to obtain acceptable results that would result in no money having been saved. Hence, they were ripe to hear yet another alternative. Consider this simple solution: Hire a consultant to come in for one day, ask some high level dumb questions and, based upon the answers, try a very limited round of recommended changes. The fee would be just one day's consulting engagement and payment would also be based upon results. Thus, for a very small fixed cost and one additional day's effort, they could possibly salvage the project budget and, at worst, for no cost and yet be even better prepared for the Method-R tuning attempt should they proceed.

So the consultant sat down with their DBAs and asked some questions about their application. Was it OLTP or data warehouse? What was the nature of the application's queries? Were the queries predominately pre-canned or more ad-hoc? What would the daily workload profile look like? I asked these and a host of other seemingly basic and innocuous questions. I then asked to see their configuration settings for their SAN, LUNs, operating system, kernel and database. They became quite skeptical since these were exactly the kinds of things the prior tuning effort had worked with. But the consultant explained to them that he was doing this devoid of any observed performance values. He was simply doing a brain-dead verification of the settings based upon their answers to his questions. By changing just five basic database configuration parameters, the average response time was reduced under maximum concurrent load by 99.4%!

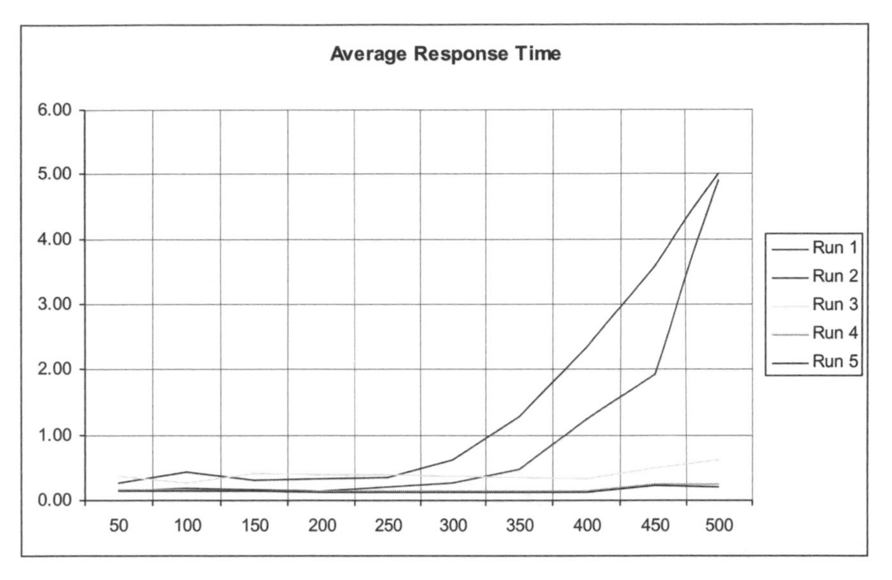

Figure 9.2: *Chart of Customer X's Adjusted Parameters*

So what great "black magic" was employed? Absolutely none – recommendations were given to adjust five basic database parameters (see Figure 9.2 above) based upon the answers to the dumb questions:

- Run 1: reduce the multi-block read count to 2
- Run 2: reduce the db block size from 8K to 4K
- Run 3: cursor space for time=true & cursor sharing=similar
- Run 4: optimizer index caching=80 and index cost adjust=20
- Run 5: maximize jumbo frames on the RAC private network

In a nutshell, their RAC interconnect traffic and delays were killing them. Since the application was a fairly standard third party OLTP application with lots of screens and reports, the settings above made sense more than the database defaults as their starting point based upon the 50,000 foot vantage point. Common sense or wisdom was the guide – not some off-kilter database ratio or metric.

So in reality, it is obvious that all the consultant did was to apply experience based, pre-emptive Method-R via abstract reasoning upon their answers. But this step is often skipped by many DBAs. In this case, a satisfactory answer was obtained for one twentieth the cost and one day's time. Customer X was actually able to skip the Method-R consulting engagement and successfully deploy the application.

The key point here is that tuning can be stopped whenever the SLAs are met, and anywhere along the three-step process.

Virtualization Wrinkles

So how well does this simple three-step process for database tuning and optimization work in the virtual world? Review the steps:

1. Ask a lot of high level, dumb questions, and verify the basics
2. Perform *Method*-R like database application trace file analysis
3. Perform a final database "health check" using diagnostic software

The first step relies on a DBA's wisdom or experience-based insights. Since virtualization, and particularly Oracle databases on virtual servers, is so relatively immature, this step is not as reliable. There is not sufficient empirical evidence to support making too many preemptive tuning strikes. But here are some best practices worth checking at this stage of the process, i.e. high-return "low hanging fruit:"

- Hardware Sizing
  - Better to have more memory rather than fastest CPUs
  - Consider adding inexpensive NIC per virtual machine
  - Ponder spreading virtual machine I/O across controllers

- Workload Related
    - Are the cumulative co-hosted virtual machines' workloads characteristics compatible and well balanced?
    - Is each of the co-hosted virtual machines' configuration properties proportioned for concurrency?
    - Are too many of the co-hosted virtual machines' configuration properties using multiple virtual processors? (estimated 20-30% overhead /VM doing so)
- Database Related
    - Do the database configuration parameters match the current properties for virtual machine? (e.g. SGA size, CPU count, DB Writers, I/O Slaves, threads/CPU, etc)
    - Are the cumulative co-hosted virtual machines' database configuration parameters reasonably defined?
    - Are the cumulative co-hosted virtual machines' database workloads compatible and sensibly balanced?

The second step of implementing Method-R based instrumentation analysis is essentially unchanged. However, there are two small wrinkles to take into account. First, treat multi-database virtual machines on a single physical server as single machines running with multiple instances would have historically been treated, i.e. examine the trace in terms of the multi-database context. While there is not a truly reliable direct correspondence between these two scenarios, the basic logic and corrections for multi-instance tuning can often apply to the virtual world or at least provide a sound starting point. This allows the application of more historical know-how.

Second and more critically, Method-R attempts to eliminate *skew* during database performance analysis. Skew is the measure of non-uniformity in a set of performance related data and is often non-obvious, uncorrelated and can lead to incorrect tuning and optimization conclusions. The problem is that virtualization by its very nature complicates process monitoring in general and especially instrumentation. The virtual machine's system clock will not be 100% accurate due to time drift inherent with this architecture, i.e. client OS system clock actually accessing abstracted hardware and future time sliced by the host. Thus, the actual run and wait time values may be slightly off. However, their proportional ratios should be fairly reliable. So Method-R should generally work as expected.

Third and most critically, the monitoring and diagnostic approach by computing ratios based off aggregate performance numbers is severely challenged on virtual machines. The Method-R people say that this method suffers skew due to the very aggregate nature of the numbers examined. However, with the run and wait times suffering drift, thereby making the OS times off, the database being a level higher than that and the performance data being aggregate in nature anyhow, the cumulative effect is that not only are the numbers off, they may well even be disproportionately incorrect. So the fancy dashboards and complex scripts could well provide totally unreliable observations such as yielding flawed conclusions, even more so than the Method-R advocates normally attribute. Of all the steps, meaning the methods for database optimization and tuning, this one should be even further reduced in importance than normal. That is not to say that the tools will not work, only that they are even more challenged than normal. So use such tools with an additional level of skepticism and doubt in the virtual world.

Special Note: This time, drift issue on virtual machines may also skew Oracle Stats Pack and ADDM/AWR reports. It may also potentially negatively affect other Oracle items, such as TKPROF, trace files, SQL*Plus timing, Performance Analyzer, Real Application Testing and Database Reply. Essentially any performance metric, indicator, measurement, ratio or calculation based upon the system clock may be slightly off. Only hard numbers remain totally unaffected, such as run queue length, memory used, memory free, I/O counts, paging occurrences, swapping occurrences, etc. So be extra careful.

Interesting Possibilities

One of the neatest things that virtualization offers the DBA trying to optimize or tune a database is the ability to leverage the flexibility of virtual machines to make some interesting possibilities a reality. Some of the more common examples will be examined here.

Divine Isolationism

In politics it may be a fundamental mistake to practice isolationism, but for database tuning efforts, it might yield substantial insights otherwise not available. Assume there are two databases, X and Y, on one physical server and that one or both are having problems. Now the DBA could try to tune the problematic databases in place, or just as easily relocate one of the virtual machines to another server. There are two immediate benefits to this approach. First, obviously database tuning is being performed one at a time. Sometimes it is easier to tune them separately and then put them back together to see how well they play together once they have been individually tuned. Second, a problem can instantly be identified that is solely due to cohabitation. If either database performs acceptably after the relocation, then the performance problem (or at least the bulk of it) can be ascribed to sharing that server.

Dueling Databases

Sometimes two databases will behave perfectly fine when isolated but cannot seem to cohabitate on one server. So in that case, the options are to either separate them or try to optimize the underlying problem by tuning them in conjunction. That means they must be tuned together or relocated permanently away from each other. Assuming the DBA tries to tune them together. The result is an interesting challenge that is reminiscent of the mythical pushmi-pullyu beast from the 1967 version of Dr. Doolittle. Yes, I am dating myself!

There is a reason for bringing this up. It is not clear how a llama with two front ends was supposed to walk. Likewise, it is not clear what the value in cohabitation is if it is simply easier and cheaper to relocate. That is the real beauty behind database virtualization. Servers can be treated as nothing more than general purpose resource pools. When one pool seems uncomfortable, too full or otherwise unfriendly, just move on.

Upgrade Heaven

A serious and often unnerving task many DBAs face at some point is that of hardware upgrades. In the old days, that almost always meant that something significant was changing that would affect the Oracle database. For example, moving the Windows database server from an Intel based motherboard to an AMD based one. Many times, changes like these would require properly moving the database from one platform to another and often with some platform specific issues to address. But with virtualization, that problem is avoided most of the time now. Since the hardware has been abstracted or virtualized, the database can be relocated and up and running by simply restarting the virtual machine. This one item alone may free up a few three-day weekends spent doing such upgrades.

RAC Smack Down

With the general consensus being that RAC is only as strong as its weakest link, namely the interconnect, many DBAs spend inordinate amounts of time trying to completely tune that one aspect of their cluster. Sometimes they spend so much time on this one item that they do not move on to other more pressing issues. So here is where virtualization can assist RAC optimization efforts. It is not advisable to deploy a RAC setup where one physical server hosts multiple RAC nodes/instances. But it can be done with the benefit being that there will actually be no interconnect going over a network, but rather all being performed in memory. So if this was tested and there was still a major performance problem, it would immediately be apparent that the problem must be somewhere other than the RAC interconnect. Being able to eliminate such issues so readily makes RAC deployment actually less fearsome. That alone makes virtualization worth serious consideration.

Distributed Nirvana

Very similar to RAC, a situation with a distributed or replicated database where performance is an issue. Once again for performance testing purposes, one option is to co-locate them to eliminate the network issue. That might more quickly lead to the often suspected bottleneck, and as a result, helps identify the true underlying problem. So, if the two-phase commits or snapshot refreshes are still having problems once the network is eliminated as the possible cause, then it must be something else. That knowledge alone is quite often worth its weight in gold. The same technique can even be used to resolve suspected DBLINK performance issues.

Dynamic Databases

It is very tough to initially size a database server's needs. Sometimes even once the database has been built, the growth rate or retention period is sometimes radically different than initially planned. So it is quite easy to over- or under-order hardware. But with virtualization and the general ability to assign resources based upon true current need, DBAs now have the ability to increase or decrease database resources via the abstraction layer. This is infinitely easier and cheaper than doing it in stand alone hardware. Therefore, a new tuning and optimization discipline emerges, that of right sizing the hardware on an ongoing basis. That is really never been feasible before.

Database Grids

I am hoping that with the adoption of virtualization, another long standing dream may finally be realized – shared corporate data. What this means is singular, centralized databases containing one true copy of mission critical data. Think of this as normalization at the highest level. I have seen many companies where the CUSTOMER table is implemented fifteen different ways within their distinct business units or lines of business. So the data architecture group gets them to agree on a standard definition, but that still results in at least fifteen tables that essentially contain the exact same data. Imagine how surprised a client would be when a financial company said that he had to send seven change-of-address cards to their various business units in order to actually completely effect the change. Needless to say, that client probably switched to a new financial company. While they are not there yet, imagine organizations actually starting to collapse all those duplicate copies of tables as "subject area" virtual machines. That would have two tremendous values to their customers: having a single copy of accurate data that can easily be changed at one time and place and the companies would benefit from reduced scrubbing/cleansing of the data between systems. As for the reduced disk space, at $50 per gigabyte, that is just not a factor for consideration.

Conclusion

This chapter examined many of the techniques, backgrounds and other diverse issue related to database optimization. There are many great papers and books on these topics and most will apply fairly well within the virtualized database world with a few minor exceptions. Furthermore, virtual databases add some interesting new wrinkles and possibilities to the equation. But through the application of a simple technique that combines the best of many other techniques, knowing when to quit, meaning that SLA has been met, and by leveraging virtualization to augment the tuning repertoire, it should be possible to successfully deploy Oracle databases of any kind on virtual servers. In fact, given some of the benefits possible, it should actually be preferred!

Oracle Virtual Appliances

CHAPTER

10

Using old Oracle techniques can be dangerous

Overview

The changes in the world of computing are genuinely amazing. These are truly exciting times because the rate of that change does not seem to be slowing down. Virtualization is just one of the many amazing new technologies that is both quickly and radically transforming the nature of the game. Physicians are lucky because the human body mutates so slowly that they have a relatively easy time keeping up with the fundamental changes in their field!

One of the central theses of this book has been that virtualization is nothing more than the logical progression of abstraction of excess resource capacity of modern hardware. Virtualization offers many benefits, most of which extend to the database management area. With virtualization quickly becoming so mainstream, there are going to be many more new and interesting developments peculiar to the database world. So here are some of the possibilities.

Software Delivery

The time honored method of delivering commercial third party applications or software has generally been to create media (e.g. CD/DVD) containing platform specific executable images with appropriate installation utilities and documentation. It has then been up to the customer to read that documentation thoroughly, prepare the platform to accommodate that new software, i.e. apply updates and/or patches, set required configuration options and run the installation utilities. That may seem like a straightforward and easy process. But as any software vendor will say – no matter how simple they think they have made it, it is nonetheless one of the key areas requiring technical support, and sometimes lots of it. Some applications are so autonomic in nature that once successfully installed, there is actually nothing else to do. So in those cases, the installation pain may comprise a vast majority of the tech support calls. It just seems like there has to be a better way of delivering software.

Virtualization could well become the new primary paradigm for delivering some types of software while solving these installation woes. With open source operating systems such as Linux, third party vendors can now package together some types of software in prepackaged virtual machines that are both successfully installed and optimized for general use. In other words, software delivery could truly embrace the "black box" approach so common in many other areas of life. Thus, software delivery and deployment would be nothing more than copying the virtual machine to a server with space capacity and starting it up. That would be it. Few installation or post-installation optimization tech support calls and therefore, cheaper overall intrinsic costs for developing and delivering software. Not to mention that this paradigm would make it much simpler for the hardware vendors to offer and ship a totally pre-configured system using a single standardized and generally accepted technique, which could lead to increased sales. So virtualization offers lower development and delivery costs plus the potential for greater sales. That is exactly what the doctor ordered.

Subsequently, what are some potential candidates for such software delivery specific to the database world? The following examples should be at the forefront of adopting this technique. Not only because the method offers the benefits ascribed above, but because these particular software packages are also used pervasively throughout the database world. So they offer the largest potential in terms of realizing those benefits.

Many of today's applications are structurally architected along the lines of what is shown in Table 10.1 with the grey shaded areas representing what is often refer to as an application when third party software packages are purchased and deployed. For the sake of example, assume this involves a fictitious ERP application – which will be called **BERP**, for "Bogus ERP."

Generic Application Tiers			
Presentation		Application	Data
Web Browser Client Apps	Web Server Report Server	App Server Mail Server Messaging Server Scheduler	Database

Table 10.1: *Generic Application Tiers for BERP*

Currently, the vendor supplied software manual describes two ways to deploy BERP: a single server vs. a single server per tier. Assume that many people will choose the latter scenario for perceived performance reasons, i.e. distribute the load across three servers. So the basic installation process might read something like this:

1. Install OS on presentation server
2. Perform basic OS optimization and tuning
3. Perform specific OS optimization for web server usage
4. Install web server
5. Perform basic web server optimization and tuning
6. Run BERP script to install and optimize its web server components
7. Install OS on application server
8. Perform basic OS optimization and tuning
9. Perform specific OS optimization for app server usage
10. Install app server components/infrastructure
11. Perform basic app component optimization and tuning
12. Run BERP script to install and optimize its app server components
13. Install OS on data server
14. Perform basic OS optimization and tuning
15. Perform specific OS optimization for data server usage
16. Install database (e.g. Oracle)
17. Perform basic database optimization and tuning
18. Run BERP script to install and optimize its database server components, objects and base data

Whew, that is a long and tedious process! Plus, there are many points along the way for users to ask ancillary questions such as what OS for each tier, what basic OS tuning they recommend, what version of the application server components and why, what database version, etc. Now imagine that BERP is delivered on two sets of DVDs instead. The first set contains a virtual machine for the single server setup and the second set for the multi-server setup. Users just need to copy the chosen VM architecture to their respective servers and press start. That is much less work for the user, which can lead to improved initial impressions and that is very important.

Content Delivery

While this scenario may not currently be quite as common, it is increasingly becoming much less unusual. Sometimes customers will buy third party reference data to support their own applications or even to support other third party software. For example, a client might want to add a US postal verification and completion option to their bogus ERP or BERP deployment. This need is so common that it can be reused multiple times across many different applications within their company.

It would be much easier to purchase a virtual machine based product for that data that offered two methods for utilizing its data. First, it could simply be a virtual machine that serves as a self-contained application server for the business logic necessary to verify and complete address information. That way the client could deploy it once and use it many times. But many people are still uncomfortable with DBLINKs, so this might not be their first choice. But with cheap hardware these days, why not allocate a small virtual machine per application that performs this task just for that specific application? That way, the client keeps remote database access to a minimum, i.e. 1 level deep, and also does not introduce any potential cross application performance problems.

Repository Platforms

Many third party products require a repository or centralized database to record historical information, and/or to permit the management of processes from a single location. This is especially true in the database. The following covers time prevalent and almost identical product lines within the Oracle DBA support software arena.

Everyone has to do backup and recovery because data is the most important asset any company has. Many backup and recovery tools have a centralized management console and repository that they recommend setting up on a dedicated server. From there, the products often deploy light weight agents on the servers being serviced in order to actually perform the work. In many ways, the steps to set this type of product up might be quite like the prior BERP example, which includes a lot of steps, but restricted to a single physical server this time. As before, it would be very easy to package this up as a single virtual machine and, once again, place it wherever spare capacity exists. In fact, backups might be performed just once a week, like Saturday at midnight, and then execution of that sporadic task can be load balance onto whatever server each Saturday morning has capacity to host that weekly process.

Another mission critical area is database performance, or the users' perception of it, such as response time and meeting service level agreements (SLAs). As with backup and recovery products, many Oracle monitoring and diagnostic tools have a similar architecture. It is not uncommon to also have a dedicated monitoring server for its repository and management console. But unlike backup and recovery which is generally executed on a defined schedule, performance efforts will be unpredictable as to when they will occur and how long they will last. It might be necessary to leave a monitoring dashboard up at all times. So monitoring tools cannot be relocated based upon spare capacity at the time like what was done with backup and recovery. But the monitoring and diagnostic product could be deployed as a virtual machine and that VM could be treated like any other mission critical system. Hence, it would be up at all times and be allocated a permanent slot within the resource pool.

In fact, these last two examples make so much common sense that it is this author's hope that all third party database software vendors start using this software delivery model exclusively. Maybe users should even demand it. It is a win-win scenario for both vendor and customer and it lets the DBA focus on the task instead of the technology of the product used for that task. Thus, it is truly a beneficial "black box" solution and one that could make DBA life a little better.

Application Development

An area that offers non-software vendors, i.e. companies doing their own customer specific database application development, an opportunity to leverage these same techniques are predefined database application project development environments. A central data architecture and/or database tools group might create several database version and application nature templates to support projects their company may undertake. Examples might include:

- Oracle 10g for OLTP
- Oracle 10g for Data Warehousing
- Oracle 10g for mixed usage

For each of these, they might offer different packaging options based upon the development tools to be used. So, for example, the 10g for OLTP might come with the database preconfigured for precompiler support, whereas the data warehousing solution would come with ETL tool support preconfigured. Having such templates readily available would provide two key benefits. First, it would provide a simple yet reliable mechanism for application development to quick start database application development efforts. But more importantly, it would foster enterprise level adherence to standards since all teams would start from the same virtual machine templates.

Education & Learning

Here is another area where using a virtual machine might not seem as readily apparent, but which supports all the concepts above. This scenario involves an Oracle training class and in that class they provide each student a self-contained virtual machine for doing the programming assignments and labs. The training facility gets the benefit of easy setup for each and every class, no matter what the size. The student gets the benefit of bringing the learning environment home with them. That way, the student can continue to expand upon those principles or refresh those concepts at a later date when the material is more significant to tasks at hand. And since many Oracle specialty or reference books attempt to achieve the same end result as a class, they should also include a virtual machine for the topics covered.

Book's Virtual Machine

It would be silly to express the prior opinion and then not include a virtual machine with this text. Therefore, the author has created what he hopes can serve as a useful, self-contained virtual machine for basic Oracle database learning and experimentation.

Plus, it can serve as an example of how one might construct their own library of virtual machine templates.

The DVD in this book contains a virtual machine which includes the following preinstalled and optimized for generic database usage:

- CentOS Linux 4.5, with all current patches at the time
- Oracle 10g Release 2 Express Edition (Oracle freeware)
- Oracle SQL Developer for Linux (Oracle freeware)
- Four Free or Open Source ERP products' schema objects

The following information will be necessary for using this VM:

- Linux logins
    - root/root123
    - oracle/oracle
- Oracle logins
    - sys/mgr
    - system/manager
    - dba/dba (sample DBA type account)
    - dev/dev (sample developer type account)
- Oracle Application Xpress URL
    - http://127.0.0.1/apex
- SQL Developer install location
    - /opt/sqldeveloper
- Oracle RDBMS install location
    - /usr/lib/oracle/xe/app/oracle/product/10.2.0

More about the Open Source ERP products can be obtained from:

- www.compiere.com
- www.opentaps.org
- www.openbravo.com
- www.sdc.ca

Below in Figures 10.1 and 10.2 are screen snapshots showing the database up and running and being inspected via SQL Developer and Oracle Application Express (which has been set as the web browser's default home and bookmarked as well):

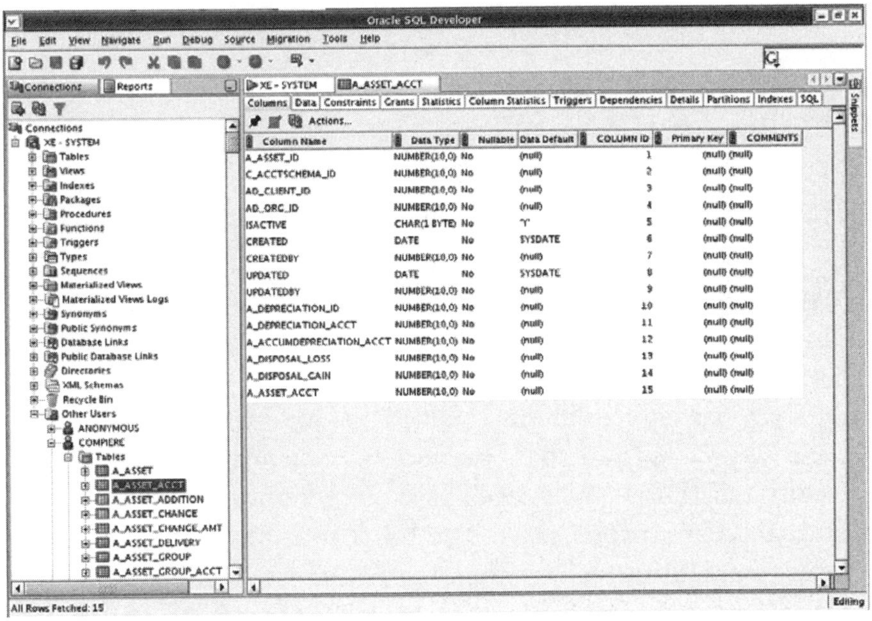

Figure 10.1: *Screen of Database in SQL Developer*

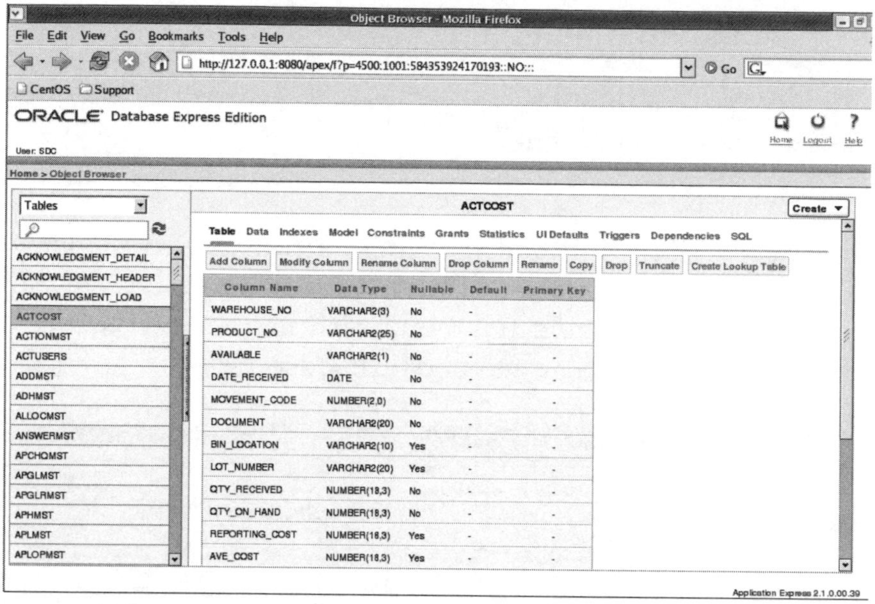

Figure 10.2: *Screen of Database in Oracle Application Express*

Conclusion

This chapter examined the many possibilities of using Oracle database virtual machines. It is not just an interesting and exciting technology; it also has numerous practical usages with the traditional DBA prevue. These techniques just need to be embraced and propagated. The book includes a DVD consisting of a template virtual machine with Oracle Express Edition (i.e. XE) and some free or open source ERP objects.

Index

T

V

X

About the Author

Bert Scalzo is a Database Architect for Quest Software and a member of the TOAD team. He has worked with Oracle databases for well over two decades, starting with version 4. His work history includes time at Oracle Education and Oracle Consulting, plus he holds several Oracle Masters certifications. Mr. Scalzo also has an extensive academic background - including a BS, MS and PhD in Computer Science, an MBA and several insurance industry designations.

Mr. Scalzo is an accomplished speaker and has presented at numerous Oracle conferences and user groups - including OOW, ODTUG, IOUGA, OAUG, RMOUG, et al. His key areas of DBA interest are Data Modeling, Database Benchmarking, Database Tuning & Optimization, Star Schema Data Warehouses and Linux. Mr. Scalzo has written articles for Oracle's Technology Network (OTN), Oracle Magazine, Oracle Informant, PC Week (eWeek), Dell PowerEdge Magazine, The Linux Journal, www.linux.com, and www.orafaq.com.

He also has written six books; *Oracle DBA Guide to Data Warehousing and Star Schemas*, *TOAD Handbook*, *TOAD Pocket Reference* (2nd Edition), *Database Benchmarking: Practical Methods for Oracle 10g & SQL Server 2005*, *Oracle on VMware: Expert Tips for Database Virtualization*, and *Advanced Oracle Utilities: The Definitive Reference.* Mr. Scalzo can be reached via email at bert.scalzo@quest.com or bert.scalzo@yahoo.com.

About Mike Reed

When he first started drawing, Mike Reed drew just to amuse himself. It wasn't long, though, before he knew he wanted to be an artist. Today he does illustrations for children's books, magazines, catalogs, and ads.

He also teaches illustration at the College of Visual Art in St. Paul, Minnesota. Mike Reed says, "Making pictures is like acting — you can paint yourself into the action." He often paints on the computer, but he also draws in pen and ink and paints in acrylics. He feels that learning to draw well is the key to being a successful artist.

Mike is regarded as one of the nation's premier illustrators and is the creator of the popular "Flame Warriors" illustrations at www.flamewarriors.com, a website devoted to Internet insults. "To enter his Flame Warriors site is sort of like entering a hellish Sesame Street populated by Oscar the Grouch and 83 of his relatives." – Los Angeles Times.
(http://redwing.hutman.net/%7Emreed/warriorshtm/lat.htm)

Mike Reed has always enjoyed reading. As a young child, he liked the Dr. Seuss books. Later, he started reading biographies and war stories. One reason why he feels lucky to be an illustrator is because he can listen to books on tape while he works. Mike is available to provide custom illustrations for all manner of publications at reasonable prices. Mike can be reached at www.mikereedillustration.com.

Need more horsepower?

Call the Oracle Experts.

On-Site Oracle Training

- Oracle RAC and Grid Training
- Oracle 10g Expert Secrets
- Customized Oracle Training
- Follow-up Mentoring

Expert Oracle Support

- Remote DBA
- Remote Oracle Health Checks
- Oracle Tuning
- RAC & Grid Support

Burleson Oracle Training is the top choice for on-site custom Oracle training and support. You need real Oracle experts, experienced professionals who can get to the heart of any Oracle problem.

Slow Oracle Performance?

BC is a leading provider of remote Oracle Health Checks.

Join the Fortune 50 companies in choosing BC Oracle Training for your next Oracle on-site Oracle class.

Call Now

866.729.8145

www.dba-oracle.com